"Daniel has a uniq   ;
of growing up. Th₁   ....d
descriptions I have lived with Daniel from childhood until
high school graduation. Daniel has allowed me to go with
him to his farm, school and church. He has helped me reflect
on God's care and guidance during those developmental
years in my own life. Excellent book."

—Rev. Ronald Bouwkamp

"Daniel's *Memoir* was a very enjoyable journey for me to be
part of as I looked in upon his life to glimpse a child and
young man's discovery of the world around him. Daniel's
style of writing provided an immediate sense of warmth
and intimacy, making it easy to imagine what it was like
to experience the events and encounters of his young life.

The strongest affirmation I can give of *The Flying Farm
Boy* is that each chapter could easily become story themes
for a year's worth of programming by Garrison Keillor. In
fact, it was delightful for me to imagine how Keillor might
take and expand upon each of Daniel's stories, adding
more 'truth' to the already-delightful telling of childhood
adventures.

I probably got more enjoyment out of the book than
Daniel intended due to my own flights of fancy but, then
again, his style of writing lends itself to the reader entering
into the emotion and feelings of his experiences. Books like
this give welcome enjoyment, enhanced perspective and
deeper appreciation to life."

—Dr. Nicholas V. Kroeze

THE FLYING
FARM BOY

THE FLYING FARM BOY

A MICHIGAN MEMOIR

DANIEL BOERMAN

WinePressPublishing
Great Books, Defined.

WinePress Publishing (PO Box 428, Enumclaw, WA 98022) functions only as a book publisher. As such, the ultimate design, content, editorial accuracy, and views expressed or implied in this work are those of the author.

ISBN 13: 978-1-4141-2092-8
ISBN 10: 1-4141-2092-3
Library of Congress Catalog Card Number: 2011927813

To Dad,

who was always a true farmer at heart.

CONTENTS

PREFACE

IT WAS JANUARY 30, 1951. As the day progressed the west wind grew in intensity, driving the falling snow across the barren fields. In spite of the stormy weather, Dad and Mom knew they had to make a trip to Zeeland that afternoon. They dropped off three-year-old Beverly at her Grandpa and Grandma's house, and told her she would be staying there for the next few days.

At about 5:20 that evening I entered the cold, snowy world of a Michigan winter, safely sheltered in Zeeland Hospital, and was soon cradled in the warm arms of my mother. Called into the room after the delivery was finished, Dad welcomed the birth of his first and only son. All too soon, after holding me for a time in his own arms, he had to drive back home to the farm to do his evening chores.

There were no headlines about my birth in the local papers the next morning, but for me, the beginning of life was certainly newsworthy. The story of what happened in the following years is told in the pages of this book.

THE BIRD'S-EYE VIEW

IT WAS A recurring dream. I pumped my arms vigorously and was soon soaring into the air. Dad, Mom, and my two sisters looked up in astonishment as I floated effortlessly over the house and disappeared on the other side. Circling around, I reappeared over the housetop and surveyed the farmyard scene below me. The cattle were grazing content- edly in the pasture, one of our cats was walking leisurely across the yard, and a few tall weeds stood out with obstinate clarity in the garden.

I pumped my arms a little harder to make it over the tall catalpa and box elder trees near the house, and kept an eye out for the power lines in front of the house. Flying into one of them could be deadly. I vaulted over the corn crib and floated leisurely over the expansive roof of the barn.

Usually I limited my flights to a small area around our farmyard. But occasionally I flew across the countryside for a mile or two, surveying the rectangular fields of corn, wheat, and hay and the acres of forest and uncultivated land in between. Long rows of trees separated one farm from another, and trees and buildings clustered around each farmhouse. Floating around at this height gave me a perspective quite different from the normal one on the ground.

I sometimes had frightening dreams too, like the time I was standing outside near the barn and saw a tornado coming directly toward me. I turned immediately to run toward the house and get into the basement, but my body was suddenly paralyzed. The tornado was bearing down on me and I could not move a muscle. Fortunately I woke up before the tornado hit.

But I would rather think about my dreams of flying. I always started flying at home, and the only people who ever saw me flying were my family members. I never flew over my church or my school. Can you imagine the sensation I would have created by soaring above the playground at school the way I did above our farmyard at home? I wasn't so much flying to show off or to attract attention as I was simply enjoying what I could do in my family's presence.

And what a joyful thing flying was! The sheer exhilaration of defying the law of gravity is difficult to describe. The ability to soar above the ground gave me a feeling of incredible power and rare delight. It transformed my world into a whole new experience.

Flying gave me the opportunity to enjoy a bird's-eye view of my world. In our dining room we had a picture of our farm taken from an airplane flying overhead. When I flew, I enjoyed the same view as the one from that airplane. It made everything look a little smaller and more picturesque. It suggested that someday I would be able to see our life on the farm from a different perspective. Maybe someday I would be able to soar above my childhood experience and be things and do things that were only dreams at the time. Flying expanded my horizons and opened my mind to new possibilities. If I could fly, who knew what other amazing things I might accomplish?

FLIGHT SCHOOL 101

CHAPTER 1

WHERE I'M FROM

AS MY HORIZONS expanded during my teens and twenties, I came into contact with many people from diverse backgrounds and different parts of the country. Often these people asked me, "Where are you from?" The answer I gave depended on who was asking the question. If it was someone from outside the state of Michigan, I would usually tell them I lived near Grand Rapids, because Grand Rapids was the largest city in West Michigan and often the only city in the area that my questioner would recognize.

If the questioner lived in Michigan but not in my immediate area, I might still say I lived southwest of Grand Rapids, or I might say I lived east of the city of Holland. Holland was closer to my home than Grand Rapids, but much smaller and less well-known. If someone lived in the immediate area, I might tell them I lived in Oakland, because that was the name of my community. But even those who lived only ten or fifteen miles away often did not know that Oakland existed.

Why all the confusion about where I was from? There is no easy answer. Oakland was indeed the name of the community in which I lived, but it was not a village or town shown on the map. You could drive right through Oakland and never know you had been there. Oakland was simply a farming community with no distinct center or downtown shopping area. The closest thing to a community center was 38th Street, a paved road that ran north and south. On one mile of 38th Street there was a grocery store at one end, the Christian Reformed Church close to the center, and a tiny gas station at the other end. That was as concentrated as our community became.

The road on which we lived was 144th Avenue, a gravel road that ran east and west and intersected with 38th Street at the corner on which the grocery store stood. We lived about three-quarters of a mile east of 38th Street, thus only three-quarters of a mile from the main street of our community. But even describing Oakland by naming roads such as 38th Street and 144th Avenue is more technical than we usually were at the time. We generally called 38th Street "the Church road" since our church was its most prominent feature. The road just east of our farm was "Albert Schreur's road" because the Albert Schreur family was the only family that lived on that mile. Our designations were more descriptive than they were precise.

Oakland had no post office or telephone company or stores for shopping. As long as Oakland had its own grocery store we bought our groceries there, but all of our shopping for clothes or anything else had to be done in a nearby city. This was most often Holland, a good-sized city about twelve miles west of us near Lake Michigan.

While residing in the community of Oakland we had a Hamilton address: Rural Route #1, Hamilton, Michigan. That was it. We didn't use street addresses until much later.

Since we had a Hamilton address, I sometimes said I was from Hamilton, but Hamilton was a small town several miles southwest of Oakland. Thus I could hardly claim to be a resident of Hamilton. We had a Drenthe telephone exchange, but Drenthe was a small village a few miles north of Oakland. I didn't actually live in Drenthe and besides, who had ever heard of Drenthe, anyway? What point was there in claiming to be a resident there? When we registered to vote, we did so as residents of Overisel Township, which was part of Allegan County. So maybe now you can understand why it's difficult to explain where I am from. I could claim to be from Oakland, Drenthe, Hamilton, Overisel, Allegan, Holland, Grand Rapids, or simply from Michigan, and all would be at least partially true.

If all of this sounds confusing, it was clear and simple to me at the time. Living in Oakland was obviously different than living in a large city like Detroit or Chicago. But Oakland was my home community, and I was perfectly content with that. Being a country boy was as natural to me as eating breakfast or taking a walk in the woods.

If you had visited my boyhood family, you would have found an old, wooden farmhouse set back from the road on a hill, surrounded by large trees on all sides but the front. Every few years Dad had to repaint the white, wooden siding and the black frames around the doors and windows. You would have entered the house at the back door into the back *hokje*, a Dutch word meaning compartment or cubicle, which was simply a tiny entryway that led to either the wooden steps into the basement or a door into the kitchen. The back *hokje* was crammed with the coats and hats and boots we wore while working or playing at home.

Walking into the kitchen, you would have found a long, narrow room with a washing machine at one end, a table and chairs in the center, and the sink, oven, refrigerator and a small cupboard at the far end. The kitchen walls had painted wainscot that ended at a small ledge about halfway up with wallpaper above.

One scene from that kitchen is still vivid in my mind. On a hot summer afternoon Dad and I were pitching manure out of a pig pen. At three o'clock Mom came out to the barn to tell us she had lunch ready. So Dad and I walked back to the house, took off our boots, and walked into the kitchen, where Mom had two glasses of Kool-Aid® and a plate full of cookies waiting on the table. At that time we had a wooden kitchen table and chairs that were getting worn and wobbly. Dad grabbed his glass of Kool-Aid® and started drinking it before he even sat down. As he lowered himself onto his chair while still drinking his Kool-Aid®, the back of the chair gave way and he fell onto the floor. There sat Dad on the floor surrounded by the broken pieces of the chair, still holding his glass of Kool-Aid® so firmly that he had not spilled a drop! After we all had a good laugh, Dad and I finished our Kool-Aid® and cookies and headed back to the barn to finish cleaning out the pig pen.

One door from the kitchen led to our bathroom, which featured a white, claw-foot tub and a large, white metal cabinet that held all of our towels, washcloths, and toiletries. Another doorway opened into the dining room that we used as a family room. The dining room had a built-in china cabinet on one wall and was furnished with a couch, chairs, and a floor model radio. There were three paneled doors covered with multiple coats of paint along the far wall of the dining room that led to my parents' bedroom, the living room, and the stairway upstairs.

If you were an especially close friend I might have opened the center of these three doors to reveal a steep, brown-painted wooden stairway that led to the two upstairs bedrooms. My two sisters shared the larger bedroom off to the right, while I occupied the smaller one off to the left. This bedroom had just enough room for a twin bed, a dresser, and a small chest of drawers.

My bedroom window was an old, double-hung wooden sash that rattled in its frame during a thunderstorm or a windy day. We did not have any storm windows upstairs, so it also let in a lot of cold air during the winter. To cool off during the summer, I made a special board with a few steps cut into it to prop up the bottom sash at varying heights. This allowed me to let the appropriate amount of fresh air into my room.

About fifteen feet from my window was a tall catalpa tree that produced large, white blossoms in the spring and long, spindly, bean-like fruit in the fall. Beyond that my window looked out onto the gravel yard surrounded by the corn crib, barn, and combination garage and chicken coop. When I woke in the morning, I could see which buildings had been opened up and if Dad had a tractor and plow or some other implement standing by the gas pump in front of the corn crib being readied for work in the field. On a winter morning I could look out and see if anyone had left the yard by their tracks in the snow. Sometimes during a summer night thunderstorm, I watched as the lightning suddenly lit up the whole farmyard as brightly as the noonday sun. My bedroom window was my window to the world.

Then there were those occasional nights when that window became something special; the nights when, even while sound asleep in my bed, that window became as penetrable as it was transparent, and I passed through it without a sound, soaring once again in the open sky, seeing my little world in a whole new way.

CHAPTER 2

STARTING OUT

ON A WARM spring Monday morning, Mom was busy hanging clothes on the outside lines in our backyard. Mom was a petite brunette of average height with light skin that turned to freckles when exposed to the sunshine. We had a large set of clotheslines anchored on each end by two sturdy metal pipes sunk into the ground, with a third pipe extended across the top. Between each set of pipes there were several long clotheslines. I don't know who constructed this clothesline, but it was heavy duty enough to support all of the clothes in our entire community. We used one set of pipes to support a small swing. I sat on this swing as I watched Mom take the clothes, one by one, from her large wicker basket and attach them to the line with two wooden clothespins. When she finished I pleaded, "Mom, push me!"

"Okay, but just for a minute. I have lots of work waiting in the house."

What fun it was to sail effortlessly back and forth through the air as Mom pushed me! It was a little like flying.

But soon Mom had to go back into the house to continue her work. I tried to propel myself back and forth on the swing, but I had not yet mastered that technique. Swinging was a lot more fun when Mom pushed me.

Early that evening Dad came in from the barn. He had just finished his chores. Mom sent my older sister, Bev, and me to the bathroom to wash our hands. Soon we were all seated around the kitchen table for supper. Dad opened the meal by repeating his usual supper-time prayer. As we ate, I watched Grandpa Boerman (Dad's father) carefully lift a forkful of food to his mouth. Every forkful was a challenge for his trembling hand. Sometimes the food fell off before it got to his mouth. The times when he successfully got a forkful of food into his mouth, he often coughed and sputtered as it went down. His grizzled face winced and contorted as it tried to accommodate the nourishment he needed.

Grandpa Boerman had lost the second of his two wives and was no longer able to care for himself. So he stayed with us for several months until he was hospitalized and passed away. Grandpa Boerman died when I was only three.

That evening Dad was sitting on the couch in the dining room reading his *Michigan Farmer*. I trotted up with my *Digger Dan* book. "Dad, can you read to me?"

"You want to hear that story again?"

"Yeah, it's my favorite!"

"You want to listen too, Bev?"

"Sure!"

Soon Bev and I were both snuggled onto Dad's big lap so we could see the pictures of that moody old construction crane and his demanding driver, Stan the Steamshovel Man. Old Digger Dan never felt like working first thing in the morning, so Stan had to force him to get moving. But he got excited when he saw all the children watching him.

Then he proudly showed off his prowess by gulping huge chunks of earth into his bucket and depositing them into a waiting dump truck. Invariably he worked on a school or a hospital project that would somehow benefit the children whose attention he so craved.

Like my namesake Digger, I wasn't always motivated to get moving first thing in the morning. But I hoped that someday I too would be able to do something worthwhile and impressive with my life.

CHAPTER 3

NO WINGS

SHORTLY AFTER MY fourth birthday, Bev and I were packed up and sent off to stay with Uncle Earl and Aunt Juella. Aunt Juella was one of Mom's older sisters and had four children of her own, three boys older than myself and Kathy, who was a year younger than I. Uncle Earl and Aunt Juella lived on M-40 in Hamilton, a state highway with lots of cars and trucks flying past at speeds that amazed me. I had never seen anyone go down our gravel road that fast! If we were playing outside during the day and saw a semi going past, we held up one arm and pulled down to try to get the driver to blow his horn for us. Sometimes he did. And, if we were sleeping there in the summertime, we could hear the trucks and cars going past during the night through the open bedroom window.

After staying a couple weeks with Uncle Earl and Aunt Juella, we were transferred to Uncle Gil and Aunt Della. Uncle Gil was Dad's younger brother. Here we played with our cousin Paul, who was slightly older than I was, and Sue, who was a little younger. When we ate at Uncle Gil and Aunt Della's house, we always had to be careful not to put too much food on our plates, because Uncle Gil made us eat everything we took before we could leave the table. It was no fun trying to choke down a few extra forkfuls of potatoes after your cousins were already busy playing.

The initial reason that Bev and I sojourned with our uncles and aunts was the arrival of our new sister, Gayle. But Mom had a hard time recovering from the birth of her third child. She was ill for quite some time after this, and the doctors were not able to diagnose her problem. At one point she had her gall bladder removed, but that did not bring her much relief. Ever since Gayle's birth, Mom struggled with bouts of feeling tired and depressed. We never knew how Mom would be feeling at any given time.

Because of Mom's illness, Bev and I stayed with uncles and aunts for several weeks. When we did come home, we had an older woman, Mrs. Mast, who helped Mom with some of her household chores. Mrs. Mast cooked meals, did laundry, baked bread, and cleaned the house while Mom rested.

When we were settled back at home again, I watched Dad drive his tractors, feed his animals, and maintain the farm buildings. These activities inspired my imagination and shaped the kinds of play I enjoyed. Since tractors were a big part of life on the farm, pretending to drive one was a favorite activity. I had two or three toy tractors, but my largest and favorite was my John Deere. Each tractor had its own distinct sound that I produced by a carefully designed orchestration of my vocal chords, tongue, and lips. As my sister Gayle grew older, she frequently began to play with my tractors too. But I had to supervise her closely. More than once I caught her playing with a certain tractor and making the wrong sound for it. I didn't understand how she could pretend to be a serious farmer if she didn't even know what her tractor sounded like!

In addition to driving toy tractors through the house, I also constructed farmyards with various animals enclosed in fences made from my blocks. My farmyard always centered around the small wooden barn that my Grandpa Boerman had made for me. Sometimes Gayle played farm with me. Then we had to divide up all the farm tools, animals, and blocks evenly so that each of us could then construct our own farmyard with our half of the toys. The two most prized possessions were the John Deere tractor and a large white horse. Each of us got one or the other of these two. Then we divided up everything else, and both constructed the best farmyard we could. Mom was supportive of this activity, and she allowed a nice farmyard to stay intact for a few days before we had to take everything down.

Dad and Mom also bought me a set of Tinker Toys®. After first figuring out how to assemble some of the items shown in the instructions, I soon learned how to design and build my own models. When they saw how much I enjoyed this small set, Dad and Mom bought me a much larger one. The possibilities for design and construction were endless, and I spent countless hours constructing farm equipment, cranes, trucks, and airplanes. My Tinker Toys® became an essential part of my young life.

Once I spent a long time building a large Tinker Toy® airplane. When it was finally finished, I proudly went to show it to Mom. "Look at my airplane, Mom!"

"Where are the wings?"

Looking at my airplane, I discovered to my amazement and chagrin that I had forgotten to put wings on my plane! I don't know how I thought my airplane would be able to fly. So I did make a few mistakes. But I can't imagine how I would have survived without my Tinker Toys®.

CHAPTER 4

THE FARM

I WAS BUSY riding my tricycle around the yard when Dad returned from the field with the Co-op tractor and cultivator. He had just finished cultivating a field of corn. He drove the Co-op into the corncrib and walked to the house, where he pulled his rubbers over his shoes. Then he started walking toward the barn. "Wanna help with the chores tonight, son?"

"Sure!"

Dad was a lanky, six-foot-three-inch Dutch farmer with dark hair and a ready smile. I was happy to trail along to the barn with him, imagining that my assistance was actually an important element in the completion of the daily evening chores.

First we went to feed the pigs in the west part of the barn. There were four sows with young piglets enclosed in four small separate pens. Each sow got a pail of slop, which consisted of two small tins of dry feed mixed with water. I put the appropriate amounts of feed and water into a pail and stirred it up with a large wooden stick. At first it was hard to move the stick through the thick, heavy feed, but gradually it loosened up until it formed a more uniform, thick liquid. At that point Dad grabbed the pail, gave it a couple quick stirs and poured it into a wooden box nailed in the corner of each sow's pen. Dad had to get the slop poured as quickly as possible so the feed didn't settle into the bottom of the pail. If that happened it would stick in the pail rather than pour out into the box.

Before the slop even made it into her box, the sow had her snout there waiting for her supper, and as soon as the slop hit the box she started gulping it down like she hadn't been fed in weeks. She had the whole pail-full gone in just a few minutes, licking the corners of her box to make sure she didn't miss even the tiniest bit.

While I prepared the slop for the sows, Dad ran a hose into a barrel that kept a pen of feeder pigs supplied with water, and threw some straw into all of the pens for bedding. After turning off the water hose and giving slop to the last sow, we left that part of the barn.

Next we climbed up a ladder into the loft to throw down some straw and hay bales. During the summer we packed the loft with straw and hay for a food and bedding supply throughout the rest of the year. Every few days Dad had to throw down a few more bales to replenish the supply. I was too small to handle a bale of straw or hay at that point, but it was fun to explore the expansive loft while Dad did the work. One of our mother cats had a litter of kittens in a small recess between some of the bales. So I took the opportunity to pet these tiny kittens while Dad was busy and the mother cat was away.

After this we went into the stable, where Dad first gave some dry feed to the milk cows. Then he grabbed his milk pail and began milking the first cow, squeezing the large teats to release their milk in concentrated streams into the pail. Our granny cat was sitting a few feet away watching. "Want some milk?" Dad asked her. He pointed one of the cow's teats toward the cat, squeezed it, and sent a stream of warm milk directly at the cat. The cat took aim, opened her mouth, and gulped down the milk as it streamed toward her. It was the perfect treat for a cat.

Dad proceeded to milk our four cows in turn. Most of the milk he deposited into a large, upright milk can that awaited the coming of the milkman, but a couple times a week he took a full pail to the house. There Mom put it into our pasteurizer in the kitchen before filling a few bottles and storing it in the refrigerator until our next meal. After giving some hay to the milk cows and feeding a few calves in the front of the stable, Dad took his manure fork, scooped the cattle droppings out of the gutter behind them, and threw them out a small opening in the outside wall onto a manure pile outside. He gave the cows some fresh straw, and we were done with the cattle.

The last stop was the chicken coop, where we had to gather eggs. Dad held the egg basket in one hand and used his other hand to gather three or four eggs at a time. I picked up eggs one at a time with my two hands and put them into the basket along with the ones Dad already had there. The eggs were all deposited in a series of nests, which were small wooden boxes built along the wall. The boxes had a roost in front for the chickens to land on, and were just large enough for them to sit in while they laid their eggs. After gathering all the eggs our chores were done, so we walked together to the house to see what Mom had prepared for supper.

In those early days, Dad earned a living for his family on his eighty-acre farm and the raising of pigs, cattle, and chickens. But it gradually became evident that eighty acres of corn, wheat, and hay, and the animals he could house in our barn and chicken coop were not enough. At one point Dad built an additional chicken coop onto the back of our barn, and later he expanded the west side of the barn and installed farrowing crates, which confined sows in a narrow metal crate while they gave birth to and nursed their piglets. Dad also rented land from the people who lived across the road from us, and from Grandpa and Grandma Ver Beek, who lived about a half mile west of our farm. There were also times when Dad had additional chickens at both of their farms and at our Uncle Ken's farm, which was just west of ours. He was always trying to expand his farming operation to meet the needs of his growing family.

CHAPTER 5

THE APPLE PEELER

EVERY SEPTEMBER A large truck loaded with coal appeared in our yard. With Dad guiding him, the driver slowly backed up along the east side of the house. There was just enough room for him to fit between the house and the box elder tree. When he had backed into the right spot, Dad held up his hand and shouted "Stop!" Then Dad removed a small basement window so the coal man could shovel the coal into the basement. First the coal man spread a large canvas on the ground, let down the tailgate of the truck, and watched as the coal began to fall onto the canvas. Then he started shoveling it into the basement.

In the meantime Dad made sure the door to the kitchen was closed snugly, then descended the wooden steps into the basement. Our entire basement consisted of only one room about twelve feet wide and twenty-four feet long. Its sides were constructed of stone and mortar, which was always breaking off and falling to the floor. On the far end of the basement was an old octopus furnace that dominated the whole room like a seven-foot giant trying to stand up in a child's playhouse. Along one wall was a set of wooden shelves for canned goods that were nearly full of strawberries, peaches, tomatoes, and beans at this time of year. At the near end was a small washer that cleaned our eggs. It was just large enough to contain a basket full of eggs. When washing the eggs, we set the basket inside the washer, filled it with water, then turned on the machine. A system of small pipes with nozzles surrounded the basket of eggs and sprayed them with warm water while it propelled them in a circular direction. If we were lucky, all of the eggs emerged from this bath perfectly clean and without any broken shells.

In the center of the basement was an old wooden kitchen table that we used for packing our eggs. After the eggs were clean and dried, we set the basket on one end of the table, filled a cardboard tray with eggs, and then lifted the tray into a waiting crate. Somewhere on that table there was also an ancient radio that often produced as much static as music. But an occasional strike with my fist kept it working most of the time. When I was a little older I sang along to such songs as "Big John" and enjoyed the drama of boxing matches between Cassius Clay and Sonny Liston while packing eggs.

In preparation for our load of coal, we had draped an old bed sheet over the canned goods and another one over the egg washer. We pushed the table into a corner between the furnace and the shelves. Then, as the coal entered on one end through the window, Dad shoveled it toward the far end of the basement until the one long side of the room was completely filled with coal. The result was that our basement was now only six feet instead of twelve feet wide. Everything in it was covered with a thick layer of black coal dust. Dad himself emerged from the basement looking like a veteran coal miner from West Virginia. But he was happy that our fuel supply for the winter was in place once again.

During the winter we always kept a half-bushel basket of apples upstairs in the hallway between our bedrooms. Outside the snow might be falling with a bitter winter wind whipping around our farmhouse. But the old furnace was busy transforming that pile of coal in the basement into the warm air that kept our dining room well up into the seventy degree range. Dad would often relax in his favorite chair, while Mom folded laundry in the kitchen, and we kids were occupied with our toys. But then I thought of those apples upstairs. A freshly peeled apple would sure taste good!

"Dad, can you peel some apples for us?"

"Can you get them for me?"

"Okay."

I trotted into the kitchen, got out a large bowl and our indispensable Pioneer paring knife, and headed upstairs. There I quickly piled several apples into the bowl and hurried back down the steps so I wouldn't turn as cold as the apples I was carrying. Then I eagerly presented the bowl full of apples to Dad, and he proceeded to peel and quarter them. Dad always tried to peel one entire apple without breaking the peeling so that it would end up in one circling red strip from top to bottom. And he had to peel pretty fast to keep up with the demand from four eager hands and mouths, not to mention the occasional piece he slipped into his own mouth.

When all the apples were peeled and consumed, Dad asked me to take the cores and peelings away. So I carried the bowl to a ledge along our basement steps, where we kept a large metal bowl with potato peelings and other food scraps. Every few days we brought this bowl of scraps to the pigs, where they squealed and fought over their rights to the food we had discarded. As long as we had pigs on our farm, we never had to worry about garbage disposal.

CHAPTER 6

GRANDMA'S PICNIC

ONE EVENING DAD said to me, "We need to get our haircuts tonight." Mom checked me out to make sure my clothes were clean and presentable and told me to wash my face in the bathroom. Then Dad and I were off to get our haircuts at Uncle Nick's. The ride to Uncle Nick's went through the woods and over a river, so there was always a lot to see as I looked out the car window. As our car climbed up onto the bridge, the planks on the bridge rumbled and the metal frame creaked. I peered out the window to see if I could see any fish or other creatures in or around the water.

Soon we arrived at Uncle Nick's. He lived in a small white farmhouse surrounded by a yard full of rabbits. These were domesticated rabbits that Uncle Nick had allowed to roam freely. This meant he didn't have to mow or maintain his lawn, but it resulted in a yard full of tunnels and piles of sand. There were always a few rabbits standing at the top of their burrows that would quickly duck from sight as soon as we got out of our car.

Uncle Nick was my great uncle, a brother of my Grandma on my mother's side. He had a small barber shop in the basement of his house. Once downstairs, he seated me in his barber's chair and proceeded to tickle me with his shears as he slowly reduced my mop of red hair to more manageable proportions.

When I was finished, Dad had his turn in the barber chair. I watched as Uncle Nick slowly trimmed Dad's hair all the way around his head and thinned out the top. Next he mixed some lather in his old shaving mug and spread it around Dad's ears and neck. Then he took out a large straight-edge and rapidly swiped it back and forth several times against a large leather strap hanging on the side of the chair. I stared nervously at the scene before me. Here stood a large older man with a freshly sharpened knife over my Dad, whose neck had been prepped with a layer of white foam. But then I gradually relaxed as Uncle Nick gently ran his straight edge over Dad's sideburns and his neck, carefully working around his ears. After all the white foam and the hairs were gone, Uncle Nick wiped Dad clean with a towel, and he emerged looking like he was ready for church on Sunday morning.

My Grandma Ver Beek, Uncle Nick's sister, lived with Grandpa on their farm just a half mile down the road from us. Every spring Grandma invited over all the grandchildren to take a walk with her in the woods. After she had assembled the grandchildren—usually a group of about eight to ten—she carried her picnic basket and led us to the old cattle lane at the edge of their farm. As we proceeded down the lane to the woods, we walked over the fresh spring grass and carefully made our way around a few thorny bull thistles still standing from the previous summer, always keeping our eyes out for spring wildflowers.

Once in the woods, Grandma found a grassy spot, where she spread out a large blanket and opened her picnic basket. We enjoyed the bologna sandwiches, sugar cookies, and Kool-Aid® she brought along. Food eaten outside always tasted better.

Next we visited the frog pond. My cousins, Norm and Kerry, and I competed to see who could catch the most frogs. First we scanned the edge of the pond to discover a speckled green frog hiding in the grass. Then we had to quietly creep up on him and surprise him with a quick movement of our hand to cover him up before he jumped back into the pond and swam away.

After I had a frog in my hands, I approached Vonnie or another girl cousin, tried to get her attention, then suddenly released the frog as close to her face as possible. With a little luck, the frog jumped directly toward Vonnie's face, sending her away squealing in girlish terror. After enough of these incidents Grandma rebuked us, "*Niet zo gek!*" Our aberrant behavior subsided for a few minutes until Grandma was preoccupied with something else, and the next frog became the unwilling pawn in another scare.

CHAPTER 7

NEW VENTURES

IT WAS A warm spring day. Dad was gone to buy fertilizer, Mom was busy cleaning the house, Bev was at school, and Gayle was taking her afternoon nap. When I was looking for a friend, and there was no one else around, I always turned to Sparkle. Sparkle was our Cocker Spaniel and the most faithful friend one could ever find. Although his name did not accurately describe his black coat of hair, it fit his personality perfectly. Sparkle was an all-around nice guy, friendly to everyone he met.

Whenever Dad took a tractor to the field, Sparkle followed him there. He trotted along behind the tractor and plow or disk or whatever implement Dad was using that day. It might be a cool spring morning or an oppressively hot summer afternoon. It didn't matter. Sparkle was always ready to go. Back and forth across the field, he followed Dad's tractor through the cold or heat, the dust raised by the disk, the fumes from the tractor, the rough ground turned up by the plow. Sparkle never wavered in his devotion. Once, Dad combined some wheat for a neighbor and left his tractor and combine in the neighbor's field for the night. Sparkle stayed there to guard them. Dad took him something to eat and drink the next morning.

But one morning Sparkle didn't get up from his spot in the garage to follow Dad's tractor to the field. Dad stopped to see what was wrong. Sparkle was sick. In the coming days Sparkle grew weaker and weaker. First he was unable to follow Dad to the field. Then he refused his food. Finally he wasn't even able to stand up anymore. Dad couldn't stand to see his old friend suffer any longer, so he carried him out to the pasture, killed him with his shotgun and gave him an honorable burial. Later Bev, Gayle, and I visited his burial site and shed a few tears for the friendly, wagging tail and the eager lick on our faces that we would never enjoy again.

Our next dog was a Rat Terrier named Koko. We picked Koko out of a litter of pups when he was just a few weeks old. Koko became a house dog as well as an outside dog. He was allowed to stay in the kitchen during the day but slept in the barn at night.

Koko was lively and full of energy. He was always up for a walk in the woods or some running and playing outside. He loved to run in circles around us, coming directly at us and then turning left or right at the last instant to avoid being caught. It still makes me tired just thinking about how fast he could run in those circles.

One summer day my sisters and I decided to build a tree house in a large, spreading maple tree on the west edge of our property. Since this was a significant distance from the house, we loaded our hammer, nails, saw, and pieces of wood into our wagon and set out down the road. Koko, of course, went along to share in this adventure. He always ran freely outside and was used to watching out for cars, so we were not concerned as we walked along the side of the road. One car approached us quite slowly, so there seemed no reason for concern. But after the car had passed we looked up and saw Koko lying on the road. We immediately rushed over and bent down calling "Koko! Koko!" His eyes opened for a moment, there was a brief perking of his ears and thumping of his tail, but then his eyes slowly closed, his head fell to the ground, and a trickle of blood ran out of his mouth. Koko was dead.

Our tree house never got built that day. We returned home with a dead dog in our wagon and with hearts as heavy as lead. That night both of our parents were gone. We waited for Dad to get home from his school board meeting before going to bed, because we were too disturbed to get to sleep without the comforting presence of at least one parent. Grief was a heavy burden to bear.

Later that summer, my sister Bev and I set our family card table at the front of our large lawn near the road. It was an old table, with its spindly wooden legs and cardboard top that sagged in the four spots where there was no support beneath it—the same top my cousin Norm and I later broke a hole through with our elbows while arm wrestling. But now it was perched near the road with a large cardboard "For Sale" sign hanging from the front.

This was our first proud venture into the world of commerce. The featured product was three quarts of freshly picked blackberries. We had a patch of blackberries that grew wild in our cow pasture. The berry bushes had enough briars on them so that the cattle did not eat them. Some years these bushes yielded enough berries so that we could pick a few quarts. So we placed them on the table for all the world to buy. The problem was that, on our gravel road, you could have counted the number of cars that went past our house in any given hour on the fingers of one hand. This was more a venture of faith than anything else. In spite of this very limited market, however, we did manage to sell a few quarts of blackberries.

One of the joys of early childhood is the freedom from the realities and concerns that burden adult life. What small child worries about finding a good job or paying the bills? But as we grew older we began to understand the importance that money had in making one's way through life. Thus it was natural that we tried to devise farm projects that enabled us to earn a little money. Then we could start a savings account that would help pay for college some day. Selling blackberries was the first of several attempts to build that savings account.

Later Dad bought me a rabbit coop that we set up in front of our barn. It was a large wooden structure with four rabbit pens on top of each other. Each pen was enclosed in wood on three sides, with a wire door on the front that let in the light and fresh air. It was a kind of apartment building for rabbits. We caught a pair of Uncle Nick's rabbits to start our rabbit family. Every day I gave the rabbits their fresh food and water. In the winter their water was frozen, and I discarded the frozen disks of ice and replaced them with warm water.

The object of the rabbit apartment building, of course, was to raise young rabbits that we could sell for meat. When the young rabbits were several weeks old, Dad took them away to be sold by the pound. Then I had the disgusting task of cleaning out the pen to get it ready for the next batch. But the pleasure of a check in the mail made it all worthwhile.

In the spring we often got a batch of chicks that we raised in a small brooder coop. During the summer we let them run outside in a fenced-in area. By fall they were ready to be butchered. Since I helped feed and water these chickens, I got a part of this profit as well. I wasn't getting rich yet, but at least I was able to start my own savings account at the bank. I hoped this was a harbinger of bigger and better things to come.

CHAPTER 8

ANOTHER BEGINNING

I WOKE UP early one morning before Mom even called me. The sparrows were chirping loudly in the catalpa tree outside my window as the morning sun filtered through its leaves. I waited anxiously for Mom's familiar "Time to get up!" to echo up the wooden steps to my bedroom.

Once the call came, I instantly jumped out of bed and put on the new blue jeans and cotton shirt Mom had laid out for me on the chair at the foot of my bed. Soon I was down the steps and in the kitchen waiting for breakfast.

"Good morning!" Mom said.

"Good Morning."

"You look sharp this morning!"

"Thanks."

In a few minutes my older sister, Bev, came down and Mom set the table for breakfast. Dad came in from doing the morning chores and led us in a brief prayer before we downed our bowls of Corn Flakes. When we were finished, Dad read a selection of Scripture and offered another prayer.

Once finished with breakfast, I found my pencil box with its two newly sharpened and still unused No. 2 yellow pencils and my brand-new box of eight Crayola® crayons, and carried them into the kitchen. Mom then handed me my very own lunch box, an oval shaped metal box with a yellow and red plaid design and a pair of handles that swiveled to the sides to clear the way for opening the lid. All that was in the box were two homemade cookies for my morning recess. So I put my pencil and Crayola® boxes carefully inside next to the cookies and I was ready to go.

Before Mom took us to school, however, Bev and I had to sit on the outside steps to our back porch so Mom could take our picture. There we sat, two skinny, red-haired kids with freckles covering our faces and arms. We both wore the clean, new clothes Mom bought for us and clutched our lunch boxes in our hands. The eager expectation of new things to learn and new kids to play with shone in the brightness of our faces and the intensity of our eyes.

Once finished with the picture, Bev and I jumped into the front seat of our 1953 blue Chevy with Mom, and we were on our way to school. In a few minutes we had traveled the two-mile distance, and Mom was pulling up in front of Pershing School. Pershing was a two-room schoolhouse with white painted siding and a large bell tower in front. It had a classroom on either side, with a large hallway down the center. The hallway was lined with benches on which we sat to remove our boots during the winter and large black hooks on the wall for our coats and hats.

Bev took my hand and led me up a set of cement steps and next a set of wooden steps and finally into the classroom on the west side. This classroom housed the Kindergarten through 4th grades. Bev introduced me to our teacher, Mrs. Brower, who then assigned me a desk where I could deposit my lunch box, pencil box, and Crayolas®. Once the morning bell rang, everyone took their seat and the school year was ready to begin.

I found myself in a class with seven other students, four girls and four boys in all. One of the girls attended our church, so I knew her a little. I had never met any of the others. Starting school meant getting to know a lot of new people as well as learning a lot of new things. But I was ready for the challenge. Soon, attending school became a comfortable routine, and I thrived as a student, taking delight in all the new things I was learning. Being successful at school was another big step forward, another move away from the confinement of my family, another achievement that brought me just a little closer to actually being able to fly.

During my kindergarten days I had only a few minutes to play on the playground in the morning before classes started and during a brief morning recess. I usually occupied that time on the merry-go-round or the teeter totters. But once I started first grade I had a longer lunch hour to spend on the playground. When the weather was suitable in the fall and spring, most of the students played softball. There was always one game for the kids from the older grades and one for the younger grades.

One day someone invited me to play softball for the first time. Somehow I got onto first base. Maybe the pitcher felt sorry for me and gave me a walk; I don't remember. I'm sure I couldn't have gotten a hit my first time at bat. Once on first base, I watched the batter to see what he would do. I knew I had to get to second base if I could. The batter hit a soft ground ball. It didn't look like it was hit hard enough for me to get to second base, so I decided to stay where I was. The shortstop fielded the ball and threw it to the first baseman. The first baseman caught the ball, stepped on first base and tagged me out.

"Why didn't you run?" the batter yelled at me.

"I didn't think I could make it!"

"You *have* to run. Didn't you know that?"

"No." I crept off the field, having learned a hard lesson. Sometimes we have to violate a rule and suffer the consequences before finding out the rule even exists.

When the weather was nice, we sometimes walked home from school in the afternoon. If I had made prior arrangements, I occasionally stayed by my cousin Kerry's house before coming home. Kerry was a year younger than me and lived on the farm just west of ours. Thus we were neighbors even though our houses were about a quarter of a mile apart. If I stayed at Kerry's house after school, I got to watch Popeye® and the Three Stooges® on television. This was a rare treat for me because we did not have a television at that time. I marveled at the exploits of Popeye and laughed at the bungling antics of Larry, Moe, and Curly. Once these shows were done I headed home for supper.

CHAPTER 9

CHURCH

EVERY SATURDAY NIGHT Dad and Mom insisted I had to take a bath. In my mind there were always more important things to do. The crane I was trying to build with my Tinker Toys® or the sand in the outside sandbox that needed grading were certainly more urgent. Besides, was I really that dirty? But they wouldn't take "No" for an answer, and eventually I found myself seated in a tub of warm, soapy water. Once there, I found fascinating things to do with my washcloth and the soap and water. I tried to capture as much air as possible in the washcloth, then pull it under the water and watch as the air bubbles escaped.

"What are you doing in there? Did you drown?" Dad's voice came through the door and reminded me that he and my sister Gayle needed a bath as well. So I had to cut short my water experiments and finish my bath.

The next morning Mom assembled all of us at the kitchen table for breakfast. After eating we took turns using the bathroom again and got dressed for church. I put on my Sunday pants and shirt, then clipped on my tie and completed the arrangement with my suit coat. When everybody was ready we all walked outside to our tan 1956 Ford®, and Dad drove us the mile and a quarter to church.

Oakland Christian Reformed Church was a brown brick building with stained glass windows, the largest and most impressive building in our community. When we arrived Dad dropped Mom and us three kids off at the front of church, then parked the car. Since Dad was a deacon, he went downstairs to the consistory room and entered the sanctuary with the other deacons and elders just before the service began. In the meantime Mom, Bev, Gayle, and I were ushered into a pew near the front of the sanctuary.

Everyone sat quietly reading the bulletin or meditating as we waited for the service to begin. Men who worked every day as farmers forking manure out of their cattle stalls were now scrubbed as clean as the insides of the pasteurizers into which their wives put the milk they brought to the house for their family's use. Mechanics whose hands were daily colored black with grease now had them scrubbed as clean as the rebuilt carburetors they installed on their customers' cars. The mischievous boys who spent their weeks contriving anguish for their mothers and teachers now sat astonishingly still. Indeed, one might almost suppose that their mothers had pressed their restless minds and muscles into place with as much rigidity as the creases on the Sunday pants they were wearing.

At 9:20 A.M. the janitor rang the ten-minute bell signaling that worship would soon begin. As I waited I contemplated the brass organ pipes in front of the sanctuary that looked like giant stalks of ripened wheat standing straight and tall in the summer sun. Then, as Jerald Ver Beek walked to the front and began playing the prelude, I was mesmerized by the majestic music flowing from those pipes. Just before 9:30, Rev. Kuizema walked in with the consistory and took his seat on one of the large upholstered chairs on the podium in front. Rev. Kuizema was an older man who was mostly bald but had a large clump of graying black hair on either side of his head.

The first part of the service consisted of singing several songs, receiving a greeting from God, and listening to Rev. Kuizema read the Ten Commandments. Then we got to the meat of the service: the long prayer and the sermon. Originally the term "long prayer" set this prayer apart from a few other prayers that were very short by comparison. The long prayer or congregational prayer was more expansive, including praise and thanksgiving as well as requests for God's blessing on the sick and others in our community and nation with obvious needs. But for Rev. Kuizema, the term "long prayer" was an accurate description because it lasted twenty to twenty-five minutes—often just as long as the sermon.

My biggest challenge through this long prayer and subsequent sermon was to stay awake or at least to maintain the appearance of being alert. Frequent prods from Mom assisted in this endeavor, but sometimes they were not enough. One Sunday morning I jerked my head to attention when I heard the concluding "Amen" to the sermon, only to discover that I had drooled a considerable trickle down the front of my suit coat. I wiped it off with my arm as nonchalantly as possible and hoped no one would notice the moist accumulation.

Once a year there were the evenings we had to prepare for *huis bezoek*. It was almost like our Saturday night preparations for Sunday church. I didn't have to take a bath, but Mom washed my face and made me put on some clean school clothes so I would look presentable. On Sundays we went to church, but on the evening of house visitation the church leaders came to us. Either the minister and an elder, or two of the elders came to visit our family. Everyone assembled in the living room. The elder exchanged a few pleasantries with Mom and Dad. Then Rev. Kuizema said a brief prayer and read a few verses of Scripture. After making a few comments on the Scripture, he asked Dad and Mom if we had regular devotions in our home and if they were satisfied with the church services. Next there was usually at least one question for each of us kids. If I was lucky it was an easy one: "Do you like your Sunday school class?" But sometimes it was more difficult: "Do you feel you are growing in your relationship to Christ?" or "Can you describe your time of personal devotions?" I wasn't about to admit that I sometimes fell asleep while kneeling by my bed to say my evening prayer. But somehow I always managed to say something that satisfied Rev. Kuizema. I was relieved when it was all over. It meant we had passed our family spiritual test for another year.

CHAPTER 10

INDOCTRINATION

DURING THE SUMMER between my 3rd and 4th grade years, when I was nine years old, a few men in our church decided to start a Cadet Club, a Christian Reformed version of Boy Scouts. We had never had a Cadet Club in Oakland before, so the news about an opening campout was exciting stuff! I had never slept in a tent before, so I borrowed a sleeping bag from my cousin Norm for the occasion. Next I threw a few clothes in a grocery bag and I was ready to go. I had a great time cooking over an open fire, playing games, and sleeping in a pup tent with my cousin Kerry.

As our campout neared its conclusion, however, events took a negative turn. I was walking over the site of the previous evening's campfire when a hidden ember from the fire somehow jumped up and lodged inside my sock. I brushed it off and pretended to be fine, but I was really hurting.

That afternoon we returned home in the back of a large truck borrowed from Mr. Van Dam, the owner of our Oakland grocery store and an associated egg business. It was a large, enclosed truck that Mr. Van Dam used for transporting his eggs. A dim light on the ceiling revealed a group of boys seated around the outside edge on the floor or on their sleeping bags. Some of the older boys decided to provide entertainment at the expense of the younger boys. One by one, they took a small boy and stripped down his pants and underwear. One large boy held up the victim while another boy at the opposite side of the truck shone his flashlight to expose the victim's private parts. The bright light of the flashlight against the shadows of the truck made the small boy stand out like a criminal forced to stand in a seated courtroom to receive his sentence. This produced a chorus of hoots and laughter from the older members of the group and terrorized silence from the younger ones. My name was mentioned as the next possible candidate for this exhibition, but the perpetrators decided we were getting too close to home and might run out of time. I was saved by the clock.

When I got home, Mom asked me if I had a good time. I said I did, but she wasn't convinced. "You look like you just got home from a funeral." So I told her what happened to my ankle, but I couldn't tell her what happened on our ride home on the truck. It was easier to talk about the bruising of my body than the scathing of my soul. Mom took me to Dr. Yff to have him look at my ankle. By this time I had developed a large blister there. He bandaged it up and told me to keep it that way for a couple weeks, until the blister broke and the skin beneath it was healed. I found out that a burn was nothing to fool around with.

Back at school that fall on a Wednesday afternoon, the slanted rays of the afternoon sun cast narrow shafts of light onto the wooden floor around me. I was seated at my desk on the far left side of the classroom, part of the fourth grade, the oldest grade in the little room.

The final bell sounded, signaling the end of the school day. I carefully placed my books inside my desk and made my way out to the hall. I always had plenty of time to complete my schoolwork during class hours, so there was never any need to take books home. Once in the large center hallway that separated the two classrooms, I pulled my jacket off one of the large black hooks that lined each side of the hallway. Then I scampered down the flight of wooden steps inside the building and the cement steps on the outside.

Once outside, I pulled my bicycle out of the collection of bikes parked in front of the school to where my cousin Kerry was waiting for me with his bike. We waited until the rest of our brothers and sisters were ready so we could all ride together. When everyone was finally together, we started down the road as a small caravan.

Since it was Wednesday night, we older students had to go to church for Catechism classes. The trip from Pershing School to Oakland Christian Reformed Church was about two miles, but it was a difficult route. We had to pedal up one very large hill. The weak-kneed and the faint of heart sometimes had to walk their bikes part of the way up Harold Bremer's hill. I tried to make sure that never happened to me.

Once at church, we had a little extra time before our Catechism class began. We usually rode around the church on a narrow cement sidewalk. On one side was the grass and on the other side the gravel parking lot. We had to stay alert to keep our bikes on the sidewalk at all times. One time while doing this I came around a corner at the same time that someone else came from the opposite direction. Our bikes collided and we both ended up sprawled on the gravel parking lot. This collision resulted in a few nasty scratches and the exchange of some words you would not find in our Catechism books. I never did figure out why Bruce Brower thought he could go counter-clockwise around the church.

When the time for class arrived, we all filed into a small classroom in the church basement. We sat on folding chairs arranged in neat rows, with five or six chairs in a row. You might think we were eggs packed neatly into a carton except that there were twenty to twenty-five of us instead of just twelve. We always sat in alphabetical order, which meant that I was in the front row right next to Sally Berens. Sally was the sweetest and smartest girl I ever met, but I always felt uncomfortable sitting next to her because she had muscular dystrophy and had difficulty walking and talking.

If someone sat in any row other than the front one, he could sometimes prop up his open Catechism book behind the back of the chair in front of him so he could see the answers. Other kids memorized just one answer, assuming that the minister would ask the questions starting with Sally and continue in order till everyone had received one question. Then, if they counted off from the beginning based on how many questions there were, they could figure out which question they would get. This sometimes worked with Rev. Kuizema, but when Rev. Jorritsma later became our minister he soon figured that system out and juggled the questions enough so that no one could count on receiving any particular one.

Reciting memorized answers to Catechism questions was always the most anxious part of the class. Once that was over we could relax a bit while the minister explained the meaning of the lesson to us. I'm not sure how much all that memorization helped us learn our Bible doctrine. Every year or two we started on a new set of questions and answers and promptly forgot the ones we had previously memorized.

Once released from Catechism, Kerry and I hopped on our bikes to return home. My older sister, Bev, had to attend the class that met after ours, so she came home later. A half mile from church and on our way home was the local grocery store owned by the Van Dam family. On Catechism mornings Mom gave me a dime and a nickel. The dime was intended for the collection taken in Catechism class and the nickel for some candy I could buy at the store. I was always very conscientious about using this money in the way my parents intended, and I questioned the honesty and piety of some kids who spent their dime on candy and gave only a nickel in the collection. Didn't they know that God expected at least a dime in the collection plate? How did they think they could get away with cheating on God? After all, look what happened to Ananias and Sapphira in the book of Acts when they tried the same thing: they died instantly because they lied to God about their donation to their church!

After purchasing our candy and depositing it into our mouths and/or pockets, Kerry and I continued our bicycle journey down the gravel road. Biking on the gravel was always more difficult than on the tar roads that led to church or school. We had to watch out for loose stones that could prove perilous. But Kerry soon arrived at his house, about a half mile down the road, and I had only a quarter mile of downhill riding to go. The only hard part was trying to make it up our steep driveway, but at least that was pretty short.

If church services, Sunday school, family devotions, Cadets, Catechism classes, and house visitation were not enough to indoctrinate us in the truth, there was always the possibility that Vacation Bible School might do the job. Our parents admittedly took a small risk when they sent us to a Bible School conducted by Uncle Bob, an evangelistic Baptist who did not share all of our Reformed theological beliefs. But they apparently thought it was worth the risk. Uncle Bob came through the area every summer and rounded up all the kids in a couple old school buses. The churches in Overisel, Bentheim, and Oakland took turns hosting these summer Bible Schools.

Uncle Bob (I don't recall ever hearing his last name) was an enthusiastic southern Baptist who rallied us all into a new level of excitement and even closed some of his messages with an altar call, something I had never witnessed before. We sang a lot of fun songs like "The Gospel Train" and "If You're Saved and You Know It." The best song, though, was the one that went: "Now when you're up you're up,/ and when you're down you're down,/but when you're only halfway up/you're neither up or down." We stood up on the "up" parts, sat down on the "down" parts, and crouched halfway between on the "halfway up" parts. First we sang the song slowly, then faster and faster until we couldn't keep up anymore. Everyone was laughing and teasing each other for getting behind by the time we finished the song. Doubtless there was some deep spiritual significance to these lyrics that my feeble mind never quite grasped.

The highlight of Bible School for me was the Bible drill. Every day, Uncle Bob picked out a Bible verse and announced it to the entire school. Everybody grasped his or her closed Bible and waited until Uncle Bob said, "Ready! Set! Go!" Then we tried to find the Bible verse as quickly as possible. Whoever thought he was the first one to find the verse stood up and started reading it loudly to assert his claim. Uncle Bob invited the individual who was actually first to come to the front and receive a prize. Here was a real chance to shine in the presence of all my peers. If only I could be the first to find that verse! But, of course, someone else always beat me to it. I always wondered if some of the winners cheated and started looking up the verse before Uncle Bob gave the signal to start.

CHAPTER 11

OF PREMATURE AGING

ONE MORNING WHEN I was ten years old, Mom took me for a ride in the family car that I will never forget. I watched the early spring scenes of muddy fields and patches of snow sail past the window of the car as if in a dream. Would I ever enjoy these familiar sights again? Would life ever be the same again? Mom was driving me to Zeeland Hospital to get my tonsils removed.

During the past years I had a lot of colds and sore throats, and Dr. Yff decided that getting my tonsils and adenoids removed was the cure. Since Dad and Mom trusted Dr. Yff to do what was best for me, they agreed that I should have this surgery. But no one asked my opinion. I felt like a lamb led to the slaughter. Being in an unconscious state while a doctor took a knife to my throat sounded terrifying. Could I really trust Dr. Yff? Did he know what he was doing? What if he slipped and cut my vocal chords or my tongue instead of my tonsils? What if the bleeding wouldn't stop? What if...I died? Who knew what awful things could happen to me once I had lost consciousness?

Mom gave me a hug and kiss, and a nurse led me by the hand into the operating room. After lying down on a table in the middle of the room, they strapped me down like an animal being prepared for sacrifice. But instead of plunging in a knife to achieve a quick kill, they devised a slow and torturous method of subduing me. They put an apparatus over my mouth and nose that held cotton batting soaked with ether. Every time I breathed, I inhaled a little more of the ether's noxious fumes. As I kept inhaling that awful smell, the fumes gradually sent me reeling into a nether world of darkness and panic.

My head began to pound with an incessant noise that grew louder and louder. I could feel myself drifting off into a dark world I dreaded to enter. I was sure I was dying, and there was nothing I could do to stop it. Never before had I so much wanted to escape and fly away. But no matter how hard I tried, I couldn't free myself from my restraints and the stifling ether smell.

The next thing I knew, I woke up in a hospital bed with the worst sore throat I had ever experienced. But I was alive! Wonder of wonders, I had survived the ordeal! I went home that same night to recover in more familiar surroundings. Alice Van Dam, who lived across the road, brought me a book of Life Savers, a small box that folded in half to reveal a series of Life Saver rolls on either side. I enjoyed sucking on them over the next few days to keep my raw throat lubricated. My recovery was rapid. My surgery was on Tuesday, and by Sunday I was back in church again.

When Mom took me back to Dr. Yff for a check-up, he presented me with a small glass bottle containing my offending tonsils suspended in clear liquid. There they were, those two little ugly culprits that had caused me all that terror and misery. Now I had them in a convenient bottle to show anyone who doubted my story. For many years we kept that bottle on display in our dining room China cabinet.

Later in the spring of that year, I was seated at my desk in the fourth-grade class at school. As the morning progressed, Mrs. Grit called each class to a small circle of chairs in front of the classroom. Starting with the kindergarten children, she went over the day's lesson while the rest of us worked to complete our individual assignments at our desks. Since we were the oldest grade in the room, the eight of us that made up the fourth grade had to wait until the afternoon to be called up front for our daily lesson.

When the morning lessons were finished, the noon bell rang to signal the start of lunch hour. Each of us hurried out to the hallway to grab our lunch pail and take it back to our desk. Once seated, the milkman—usually a seventh or eighth grade boy—came around with a large wooden case that contained the glass bottles of white or chocolate milk each of us drank with our lunches.

Once I got my lunch and my milk, I had to eat as fast as possible to try to finish before Mrs. Grit gave us permission to go outside to play. I was a slow eater, so this was often a challenge for me. If I hadn't finished my food by this time, I had two options, neither of them very appealing: I could throw the remaining food back into my lunch pail and try to explain to Mom that night why I hadn't finished my lunch, or I could stay inside while most of my classmates were outside getting started on today's softball game. So I always tried to finish on time.

On this particular day, however, I was less fascinated with the upcoming softball game than with the possibilities of what was in front of me in the immediate present. The bottle of chocolate milk I got every day came with a piece of clear cellophane around the top that was held on by a narrow strip of sticky blue paper. After pulling this strip of sticky paper and cellophane off the bottle top, I uncorked the cardboard plug on the inside of the bottle and it was ready to drink.

That strip of sticky blue paper intrigued me that day. It was sticky enough after being removed so that it might be successfully stuck to another surface. To what creative use might I put this paper? After some contemplation, I ripped the strip into two shorter lengths and stuck one onto my upper lip and one onto my chin. With this representation of facial hair I called to the surrounding students: "Look! I'm an old man!" My classmate Howard thought the idea was good enough to copy my behavior himself.

Mrs. Grit observed all of this from the front of the room. Part of a teacher's job was to make sure that innocent fun never crossed the boundary into something unruly or pernicious. Who knew to what depths of evil a young mind might sink if left unguarded? Something in this scenario didn't seem right to her; this imagining that one was much older, this presumption of transforming oneself into a mature or even aging adult.

When it was time to release the students to play outside, she announced to the class, "Daniel and Howard have to stay inside. The rest of you may go now." Her words brought sudden terror to my heart. I hastily ripped the offending strips of paper off my face, gulped down the last of my milk, and awaited my sentence. I had never before been asked to stay in on a lunch hour. What was so awful in what I had done? And what was to be the consequence?

After the rest of the students had left the room and gone outside, Mrs. Grit walked to the blackboard and wrote in large letters: "I AM NOT AN OLD MAN." Then she turned and said, "Daniel, I want you to write this one hundred times because you started this. Howard, I want you to write this fifty times."

So there I sat, writing my lines while my friends were outside playing softball in the spring sunshine. My heart was as heavy as the lead in the pencil with which I wrote. I felt ashamed for having violated a rule I didn't even know existed. I wanted to fly away out of that confining classroom, but I was bound to my desk as securely as if held there by a leg iron and chain.

FLIGHT SCHOOL 201

CHAPTER 1

THE BIG ROOM

STARTING THE FIFTH grade at Pershing School meant moving into the big room. It was called the big room not because it was larger than the other classroom, but because it housed the older students. This move represented the next stage in my education. It also meant I now had Mr. Lampen as my teacher.

The disadvantage of being in the fifth grade and in the big room was that I was now the smallest and youngest in the classroom. It was like starting out at the bottom rung of the ladder for a second time. This caused me the most problems on the softball field. In the fourth grade I could play up to the level of most other boys of the lower grades, but now I had to compete with boys two and three years older.

The worst part of this was trying to hit a fast-pitched softball. When the pitcher lobbed the ball over the plate softly, I could usually at least make contact with the ball. But when an eighth-grade boy wound up and pitched the ball as hard as he could over the plate, the ball was in the catcher's glove before I could even get a decent aim at it. I never did learn to hit a fast pitch.

Fortunately, the pitchers usually threw a couple slow pitches first to the younger batters to give us a chance. I desperately tried to hit one of those slow pitches because I was terrified to face the fast pitches. I knew I would strike out or, even worse, get hit on the head and knocked out with a fast pitch.

Once, I came to bat when Johnny Grit was playing shortstop. Johnny, the son of my former teacher, was a tall eighth-grader who enjoyed tormenting younger and smaller students. "Just pitch to him. He can't hit, anyway!" Johnny yelled to the pitcher. I dug in my heels and grasped the bat more tightly in my hands. I was determined to teach Johnny a lesson he couldn't learn in the classroom. The first pitch was too low for me to hit and was ruled a ball. The next pitch was still a slow pitch and high enough to hit. My eyes zeroed in on the ball and I swung with every ounce of energy in my small body. I belted a line drive toward left center field. Johnny jumped as high as he could, but it sailed just over his glove. I made it safely to first base with a single. The next time I came up to bat, Johnny had nothing to say.

When the weather was suitable, Pershing School sometimes had a softball game against Hawthorne School on Friday afternoon. Hawthorne was another small country school just two miles away. When we played at Hawthorne, Mr. Lampen loaded the entire team of mostly seventh and eighth-grade boys into his car. There were two or three in the front seat, four or five in the back, and the rest sat in the trunk with their legs and softball bats dangling out the back of the trunk. When Hawthorne played at our school the rest of us got to watch and cheer on our team.

We had several excellent girl softball players in our school at that time. Once when Hawthorne came to play our school, Mr. Lampen decided to have our girls play the boys' team from Hawthorne. We watched as Diane consistently baffled the Hawthorne boys with her pitches and induced them to bounce out to the shortstop or pop up to second base. When our girls came to bat, we enjoyed seeing Hazel and Linda repeatedly drive the ball deep into the outfield between two fielders and score another run or two. The end result was that our girls won the game. The Pershing girls, of course, were ecstatic, but the Hawthorne boys limped off the field like a pro team that had just been beaten by a Little League squad. I'm not sure their male egos ever fully recovered from that shock.

CHAPTER 2

LITTLE TOOT

MANY OF MY hours at home were spent in a small playroom off the dining room in our house. This was where we kept our toys and games. We also had a small record player with several 45-rpm records we played over and over again. Most of these records were songs such as "Old McDonald" and "Where Will the Dimple Be?" But the one I remember best was a dramatic narration called "Little Toot." Little Toot was a young tugboat growing up in a busy harbor, where he watched with pride as his father, Big Toot, pulled large ships into their docks and sometimes rescued them from a storm at sea. On one occasion a great storm came up on the sea, and Big Toot was gone on an important assignment. Suddenly Little Toot heard an SOS call sound across the harbor. A large ship was in danger on the open sea! Since there was no one else available to help, Little Toot decided he had to try. So he went steaming out of the harbor into the crashing waves of the storm-tossed sea, found the ship in distress, and pulled it safely into the harbor. Everyone in the harbor greeted him and acknowledged him as a hero. The final words of the record said it all: "And now you're a Big Toot, Little Toot!"

Like Little Toot, I longed for the day when I could be a hero and gain everyone's attention and admiration. But life on the farm did not offer many opportunities for heroism. One of the ways I imagined becoming a hero was picturing myself as a big game hunter. I should have known better, but when you're young anything seems possible. A small boy's imagination knows few bounds.

Every farm boy started out his hunting career with a Daisy BB gun. By simply pulling down a small handle underneath the gun, it was cocked and ready to fire. The BB was propelled out of the gun barrel by a spring when the trigger was pulled. It was so simple to operate that even the smallest boy could handle it.

Most of the time I used my BB gun for shooting target practice such as setting up a tin can on top of an old barrel and trying to knock it over. But the purpose of a BB gun on a farm was to shoot sparrows, which were an abundant nuisance. The problem was that a sparrow was a pretty wary bird, and it was difficult to get very close to one of them. Usually they would fly away before I could get within shooting range. A better strategy would have been to sit still somewhere and wait for them to fly within range toward me. But what ten-year-old boy has the patience to sit and wait for that to happen? Even when I did get close enough to take a shot, a sparrow was a very small target to hit with one tiny BB.

Another obstacle to killing sparrows with a BB gun was the weakness of the shot. Once, when I was being careless, I shot myself in the hand. It stung like crazy, but the BB didn't even penetrate my skin. I remember another time when my cousins and I were hunting sparrows at Grandpa and Grandma's house. We wounded a young sparrow and caught it in our hands. Upon examining it we found one BB lodged in its wing. The BB had not even penetrated the feathers of the bird. Because of all these limitations, birds did not have a lot to fear from my BB gun.

Occasionally Dad took me into the back part of our barn to hunt sparrows at night. This part of the barn had open doors and windows in the summertime, so birds could easily fly in and out. The ceiling consisted of old beams covered with straw. This formed a perfect nesting place for sparrows. If we went there at night we could find some of the birds at the entrance to their nest with a flashlight. The light from the flashlight blinded them temporarily and made them an easy target. It certainly wasn't very sportsmanlike, but we killed quite a few sparrows that way.

The next stage in my hunting career arrived with my Crossman pellet gun. This gun would shoot either pellets or BBs. Instead of a spring, the pellet gun used air to propel the shot. I had to pump the gun several times with a small piston that slid back and forth underneath the barrel. The more often I pumped it the more power it had. Twelve pumps was the maximum allowed. When I shot a tin can with my BB gun, the most I could do was knock it over; it would not penetrate even one side of the can. But with my pellet gun I could line up three or four cans in a row, and a BB would go through both sides of all of the cans.

The Crossman pellet gun was thus a huge advance over the Daisy BB gun. I shot and killed a few more birds with it. But it was still difficult to find many sparrows within shooting range. Using tin cans for target practice was usually more fun.

Another new endeavor at that time of life was piano lessons. Music always had an important part in our household. Mom loved to play the piano and sing, and she wanted all three of her children to learn and enjoy music too. This meant that all of us took piano lessons for at least a few years.

I began my piano lessons with a little apprehension and a lot of anticipation. I hoped that maybe someday I could become a famous pianist. Our piano teacher was Christal Broekhuis, a single woman who taught school and also played the organ and directed the choir at church. Once a week she came to our house to listen to us play the pieces we had practiced during the past week. She must have been a woman with amazing patience and tolerance! I could never have listened to all those simple pieces played over and over again, often with frequent and flagrant errors. But she was as patient and tolerant as a young mother watching her toddler learning how to walk.

I was not one of Christal's star students, but I did progress through the elementary stages of piano playing and actually enjoyed some of the pieces I mastered. Some of those old tunes are still familiar to me now; if you ask me, I can still sing (but not play!) the words and the tune of "Bill Grogan's Goat." I got to the point of being able to play a few simple hymns out of our church Psalter Hymnal, but it was always difficult for me to hit four different notes correctly at the same time. That required more coordination and concentration than I could achieve. Having reached this apparent climax of my piano playing ability, I decided to give up my piano lessons. If I was searching for a way to become a hero, it was clear that I would have to look to something other than playing the piano. Becoming a concert pianist was definitely not in my future.

Sometimes events gave me an unexpected chance to prove my ability. One winter morning when Dad got up and went to the bathroom, he found only a trickle of water coming from the bathroom faucet, and the toilet did not fill up after flushing. We were out of water. Broekhuis Brothers came over to check it out and discovered that our well and pump were broken beyond repair. We needed a whole new well. They brought over a large tank of water to keep us supplied until they could get our new well going. Then they came with their drilling rig and started pounding a new pipe deep into the earth.

I was fascinated with this impressive equipment and decided I had to build a well driller of my own. For my birthday my parents had given me a large Erector Set. This set enabled me to design and build all kinds of trucks and tractors and cranes and other construction equipment. So I got out my Erector Set and started to work. First I made a large truck with a tall rig on the back that would fold down over the cab of the truck or stand upright when in use. Then I mounted my electric motor on the back of the truck just in front of the rig, and designed a mechanism that produced an up-and-down motion that simulated the similar motion on Broekhuis Brothers' rig outside. When I plugged in my motor and engaged the appropriate gear, my well driller went up and down, pounding the floor of our dining room as it went.

Dad was so impressed with my creation that he brought it outside to show to the men who were actually drilling our well. They were impressed with it too! Although my invention was only a miniature replica of the original, I felt immeasurable pride in designing and constructing something that impressed both my Dad and these two rugged men working outside in the winter cold to drill our new well. Maybe my engineering abilities would someday be my ticket to success.

After three days of drilling, Broekhuis Brothers found an abundant flow of water. It was down in the Marshall Rock, over two hundred feet below the surface of the ground. They put in a new three-inch pipe with a submersible pump that gave us more water than we ever had before. Our old well sometimes got plugged up with sand in the screen at the bottom. The new well was in the rock and we didn't even need a screen. The water was fresh and clear and great for drinking. People who drank water from that well often complimented us on how great it tasted.

CHAPTER 3

THE MORON STORY

IT WAS A hot Saturday in July. Dad finished his evening chores early while Mom had a casserole cooking in the oven. Mom and Dad had promised us we could go to Dumont Lake that night if we all got our baths finished before five o'clock. After my two sisters and I met that deadline, Dad and I went to the garage and hauled out two large inner tubes. Dad pumped just the right amount of air into both of them with his air compressor, then loaded them in the trunk of the car. Meanwhile, Mom wrapped her casserole dish in several layers of newspaper and put it in a box. She put our dishes, silverware, and a few other necessities into her wicker picnic basket. We put on our swimsuits under our regular clothes, grabbed some bath towels, and climbed into the car.

Dumont Lake was a small lake several miles south of our home in Allegan County. There was a picnic area on the east side of the lake in Dumont Park. Once there, we stripped down to our bathing suits and ran across the short beach into the water. Since Dumont was a small lake the water got pretty warm in the summertime. Dad joined us in the water, and we had a great time cooling off as we splashed or floated around on one of the inner tubes. Mom kept a watchful eye from her perch on the picnic table she had claimed for us. None of us knew how to swim, but we enjoyed the cool refreshment of the water. After an hour we joined Mom at the picnic table and enjoyed her casserole together. We had worked up a good appetite!

Back at home I searched for ways to occupy my time during the summer. Sometimes I walked the quarter mile to my cousins Kerry and Danny, who then walked with me another quarter mile to Grandpa and Grandma's place. We often hunted for sparrows in their yard or played in their barn. Grandpa's barn had not been used for many years, because Grandpa had retired from farming long ago. He and Grandma worked as janitors at our church for several years, but I don't remember Grandpa ever being an active farmer. His barn was only used to store some farm machinery. This left most of it empty and ideal for exploration.

There were still several old straw bales in Grandpa's barn. We weren't big or strong enough to carry these bales around much, but we managed to move then around enough to construct forts in which we could hide from each other. Then we played cowboys and Indians, using our pointed index fingers as imaginary guns and conducting life-and-death maneuvers. There was also a long board in the barn that we managed to set up so that we could slide down it into a pile of straw at the bottom. The only hazard to this activity was the occasional sliver that made its way through our clothes and skin. After our time of hunting or playing was done, we always ended up at Grandma's kitchen table for a glass of Kool-Aid® and some homemade sugar cookies.

Kerry, Danny, and I spent a lot of time together. Sometimes we were at Grandpa and Grandma's, and sometimes we played or also slept overnight at each other's houses. Somewhere in the process of sleeping overnight we developed a peculiar institution. It was the product of the imaginary tall tale with which we tried to entertain each other. We attempted to outdo each other in telling the most astounding and ridiculous story of foolishness and stupidity. Maybe it resulted from watching too many segments of the Three Stooges together. We called these tall tales *moron stories*. The typical moron story went something like this:

One morning a moron went to the barn to do his chores. When he went to feed his cows, he saw a big horsefly flying around them. It was really bugging them, so he decided to do something about it. He went to the house and got his 12-gauge shotgun. The horsefly was flying around, so he waited until it landed in order to get a good shot at it. As soon as it landed he aimed his gun and fired. BOOM! Just as he pulled the trigger of his gun the fly took off, so the moron missed him. But the fly had been sitting right on the forehead of his cow, and the shot from the 12-gauge shotgun killed the cow.

Now the moron had to figure out how to get his dead cow out of the barn. He got out his tractor and found a chain long enough to go from the dead cow to the tractor outside. So he hooked the chain to the cow's legs and pulled it out of the barn. But he forgot to open the door far enough, so when the cow hit the door it pulled the whole door down and broke it to smithereens.

Next he had to decide what to do with his dead cow now that it was out of the barn. He figured he better dig a big hole to bury it, so he got out his shovel and started digging a hole in the cow pasture. It took him almost all day, but he finally had a hole that he thought was big enough. So he got on his tractor to pull the cow out to the hole. He wanted to pull the cow as close to the hole as possible and then move the tractor to the opposite side of the hole to pull the cow into it. He drove his tractor as close to the hole as he dared. As he drove alongside the hole the side caved in. The tractor started falling into the hole, and the moron fell off and into the hole. Then the tractor fell into the hole on top of him, and that was the end of the moron.

But, of course, the moron miraculously revived to experience yet another series of adventures. And the next story was sure to be more outlandish and ridiculous than the last.

CHAPTER 4

THE SNOWSTORM

ONE EVENING DURING the winter it started snowing steadily and the west wind began to pick up. When my sisters and I went upstairs to bed, we could hear the wind whistling around our old farmhouse, rattling the windows and making the house creak like it was trying to find a way inside. After running up the stairs, I paused for a moment to check the thermometer at the top of the steps: 29 degrees Fahrenheit! I undressed, got my pajamas on, and dove under a pile of blankets in record time that night.

The next sound I heard was Mom's voice echoing up the steps, "Time to get up!" After thinking about it for a minute I worked up the courage to get out of my cozy cocoon and make a mad dash downstairs, hoping my feet didn't freeze to the ice-cold wooden stair steps.

"Are we gonna have school today, Mom?"

"I don't know. No announcement on the radio yet, but they're going to read all the closings again in a few minutes. So we'll have to listen."

We all huddled close to the register and tuned in to the radio. I sang along with my favorite advertisement: "Buy CLARK SUPER One Hundred Gasoline!" Then came the school closings. We listened intently as the announcer listed several other schools in the area that were closed. When we all thought we had missed our chance, we suddenly heard it—Pershing School.

"Yeah," we chorused, "we can stay home today!" It wasn't that we didn't like school; but staying home during a snowstorm was special fun.

After a bowl of Corn Flakes I ran upstairs and quickly changed my clothes. Then I decided to get out my Erector Set. I wanted to make a snowplow to attach to my John Deere tractor. After total immersion in this engineering feat for some time, I suddenly smelled a delicious aroma coming from the kitchen. "Watchya makin', Mom?"

"Come and see!"

Trotting into the kitchen, I discovered Mom and my two sisters busily engaged in cooking homemade doughnuts.

"Doughnuts!" I cheered. "Can I have one?"

"No, we just started."

I watched as Mom lowered a piece of round dough into the boiling fat. Seconds later it came out a golden brown doughnut. "Pretty neat, Mom!" Mom never made doughnuts unless we were snowed in. It was like drinking a bottle of champagne; something you did only on very special occasions.

"Know what?" asked my older sister, Bev.

"What?"

"We should take some doughnuts to Grandpa and Grandma!"

"Yeah! That would be fun. Can we go, Mom? Can we go right away?"

"Hold it just a minute," said Mom. "The doughnuts aren't even cooled off yet. Besides, that's a long ways to walk through all that snow." She looked out the window to see what the weather was like. The wind and snowfall had tapered off considerably from earlier in the morning.

"Can we go, Mom? Please? Can we go?"

"Well, it looks like the storm is mostly over. I guess it's okay, if you're careful."

"Yeah! Can we go now?"

"I guess you can still go this morning. Just wait a little while for the doughnuts to cool off. Then you can start getting dressed and I'll call Grandma so she knows you're coming. That way she can watch for you."

After waiting impatiently for the doughnuts to cool, we started putting on our clothes while Mom called Grandma. It was fun to listen to Mom talking to Grandma, because she always talked half English and half Dutch.

Getting dressed to go outside was a challenge. It was always tough to find a place for all the clothes Mom told us we had to put on. After I pulled a second pair of pants over the ones I already had on, the first pair pulled up almost to my knees. So I sat down on a chair and had my sister try to find the bottoms of my pant legs somewhere under the second one. She finally found them, but she had to pull so hard to get the first ones down that I almost fell off my chair. Next a sweatshirt, coat, stocking cap, boots, and gloves, and I was all set.

Walking down the road was an adventure. We imagined we were walking through a vast wilderness at a time when cars had not yet been invented. Our challenge was to conquer this snowy wilderness through sheer determination and brute strength. In pursuit of this goal we competed to see who could walk through the deepest drifts without getting stuck. And we had to climb the highest banks along the road to prove that we were true masters of this snowy wilderness.

Before long we were at Grandpa and Grandma's house. Grandma had been watching anxiously and opened the door for us. "Oh, oh, oh—are you okay?" She helped us unpack ourselves so we wouldn't carry all of our snowy clothes into the kitchen. Once there, we all received one of her slurpy kisses, the kind you had to wipe off with your sleeve as soon as Grandma looked the other way.

Grandpa was seated in his usual spot in his rocking chair by the window. Here he could catch a glimpse of the outside world. He had on his insulated boots, long underwear, and two sweaters to stay warm. Meanwhile, Grandma ran around in her short-sleeved dress.

Soon we were seated at the kitchen table enjoying our Kool-Aid® and a fresh doughnut. Grandpa and Grandma had a cup of coffee with their doughnut, and we watched as Grandpa poured half of his cupful onto his saucer and sipped it up from there. Then we had to have one of Grandma's sugar cookies. No visit to Grandma's house was complete without that.

"Would you like to play some Rook?" Grandma asked.

"Yeah!"

Grandpa never wanted to play, so Grandma asked us to play whenever she had the chance.

Grandma loved to play Rook, but she was a timid player. You never caught her trying to run up the bid. In fact, she usually never bid at all. But when she did, well, that meant she had a terrific hand. Of course, someone else might still outbid her and she would lose the chance to lead with her hand. But we didn't let that happen too often. Whenever Grandma bid reasonably high, everyone else mysteriously passed and Grandma got the bid. And then we knew we were in for it, because now she could play her terrific hand. But we didn't mind losing to her, because we loved our Grandma a lot.

CHAPTER 5

BEAUTY

THERE WAS A steady stream of men visiting our farm, regulars whom we came to know well—the feed man, the bread man, the grocery man, and the Watkins man. The feed man came once a week to deliver feed for our animals. The day before he came, Dad brought bags of corn and wheat to the Forest Grove Mill. I often helped Dad by holding a large burlap bag open at the top while he shoveled the corn or wheat into it. Then Dad brought these to the mill, where they ground them up with the appropriate supplements. When they were ready, the feed man delivered them on a big truck to the farm.

The bread man came every couple weeks with his van loaded with fresh breads and pastries. Sometimes he had candy treats for us kids too. Once, he was getting ready to hand me a treat when our dog Sparkle snatched the candy from his hand and swallowed it whole, wrapper and all.

Every week Mom called our local grocery store to place an order, and the grocery man delivered it the next day. Then there was the Watkins man, who showed up a few times a year. We always bought a salve from him that came in a small metal container like shoe polish comes in. That salve occupied a prominent place in our bathroom cabinet, where it was always ready for the next cut finger or scraped knee.

The first farm resident to greet these regular visitors was often our dog. The farm dog functioned as a greeter and sometimes as an alarm system, whose barking alerted us to the presence of a visitor. Soon after the death of our dog, Koko, we bought a female Rat Terrier and started raising and selling our own Rat Terriers. The female who gave birth to most of these puppies was named Beauty. She established herself as an important part of our farm for many years.

Beauty had several batches of pups, most of which we were able to sell. A small puppy has to be the most adorable creature in the whole world! It was great fun to hold and pet the tiny puppies and watch them grow. I remember watching them when they first learned to eat out of a dish. We fed them crumbs of bread soaked in milk. As they stood on the side of the dish, we watched their stomachs grow wider and wider as they ate. Sometimes they would be twice their original width by the time they were done eating. I'm surprised none of them ever burst open; they were so fat they could hardly walk.

Beauty was a lively and aggressive dog. In fact, when she got older she was sometimes mean to strangers. But she was an excellent agent for pest control around the farm. She caught lots of mice and wasn't afraid to tackle a rat or other large rodents.

Beauty was also very fast. We always had a lot of barn swallows around the farm. They frequently swooped down right in front of a cat or dog as the animal was walking across the yard. Normally the cat or dog would ignore the birds and nothing happened. But on one occasion there were two swallows that swooped down right alongside of Beauty as she was walking across the yard. Watching them closely, she suddenly lurched in their direction just as they were passing and caught both of them in her mouth. It didn't pay to mess around with Beauty.

Beauty often ran out in the fields by herself seeking adventure. She was never afraid to pursue another animal or dig down into a hole in the ground to see what was inside. I can still see the dirt flying out behind her as she dug her way into a hole burrowed into the ground. Sometimes we were afraid she would bury herself in the hole, but she always managed to get back out.

After one of her forays into the wild, Beauty returned reeking with the smell of a skunk. We washed her repeatedly, but the smell remained. Someone suggested soaking her in tomato juice; this was supposed to be the definitive cure. We did so, but even this did not help. We just had to let the smell wear off with time, and Beauty was banned from the house until her disgusting aroma had disappeared.

CHAPTER 6

THE LIVESTOCK AUCTION

A REGULAR FARMING routine is the selling of animals when they are ready for market. On our farm, when Dad sold cattle, he hired a trucker to pick them up, because they were too large to fit on his pickup. But he usually took pigs away on his own truck.

Occasionally we had to load up an old sow or boar. This was a big challenge, because these animals could be pretty large. Pigs continue to grow as long as they are alive and healthy. I remember one old boar that Dad had to load by himself, because I was too young and small at the time to offer any help. After fighting with the boar for quite some time, Dad finally got him onto his red International pickup, then quickly secured the bottom and top portions of the tailgate. The boar briefly surveyed his situation and promptly jumped over the side of the truck. While waiting another week, Dad built a top onto the back of his pickup so the boar could not get out again. This time Dad got him safely loaded and delivered to the sale. When the boar was weighed, he tipped the scales at 710 pounds. I think Dad kept that one a little too long!

Feeder pigs were small enough to be carried individually to the truck. They were piglets that were several weeks old, weaned from their mothers and used to eating solid food. We had to catch a feeder pig by one of its legs, carry it kicking and squealing by its two hind legs, and deposit it safely into the back of the pickup. When I was old enough to start helping, I found the hardest part was lifting the pig up high enough to get it over the tailgate of the pickup. Sometimes I had to swing it around to get some momentum going or use one of my legs to help boost it over.

Once the feeder pigs were in the back of the truck, they had to be cleaned. Dad was a firm believer in getting them to look their best before they were presented for sale. He got a pail of hot, soapy water and an old toilet brush and scrubbed their backs and sides. Then he took a hose, sprayed them off and let the dirty water run out the back of the truck. Finally, he threw some clean straw in with them, and you could swear that they had never touched anything dirty in their lives. They were as clean as a group of high school freshmen emerging from the showers after their gym class.

Once Dad had the feeder pigs ready to go, I often rode along with him to the Hopkins Livestock Sale. Hopkins was several miles away in Allegan County. Just before the road to Hopkins curved over a large hill past a cemetery, it came to a small stone house on the corner. That house is still standing today. When we came to the stone house, we had to turn left to go into Hopkins. When we got back home later that afternoon, Mom asked Dad how things went.

"Dan talked so much on our ride back and forth that I could hardly get a word in edgewise!"

"Yuh, I bet!" Mom laughed.

I didn't get much respect for being quiet.

All the farmers bringing feeder pigs for sale parked their pickups in a row so they were ready for the auctioneer. The auctioneer always wore a large-brimmed, light-colored hat and carried a cane. He stood on the running board of each pickup and used his cane to prod the lazy feeder pigs to stand up so prospective customers could get a better look at them. Interested parties perched on the back bumpers of the pickups or stood nearby as the auctioneer tried to bid up the price of the pigs. There were times when the price Dad was offered was so low that he bought them back and kept them till a later date or fattened them until they were ready for butchering.

When Dad brought an old sow or boar to sell, we drove into the gated area connected to the building in which the larger animals were sold. There was always a man standing at the entrance gate who let us into this area by opening and closing the gate. The man who usually did this job was about the same height as the gate. I always marveled at how such a short person could have such large, muscular arms and hands. Dad told me he was a midget. After we were inside the fenced-in area, the pig was unloaded and driven into a pen, where it was held until it was ready to be sold.

Sometimes we went inside and watched the auction sale in progress. The first thing we noticed upon entering the building was the noise. There were pigs squealing and cattle bellowing, and the men who drove them around were hollering to keep them moving in the right direction. But above all this racket there was the sound of the auctioneer's voice with his loud, repetitive appeal for an ever higher selling price. If you were looking for peace and quiet, the livestock auction was not the place to go.

As we entered the selling area, Dad and I climbed up the steps and onto the benches that were built like bleachers in a high school gymnasium into one side of the building. Opposite these benches sat the auctioneer and two other men who served as clerks. They were seated behind a large, raised counter. In the center, between the auctioneer and the audience, was a small corral through which the animals being presented for sale were paraded.

Like the outside auctioneer, the man inside also wore a large, tan hat that seemed to be a symbol of his authority. But instead of a cane, he had a large gavel that he pounded loudly at the end of each sale to signify the closing of a deal. He looked very much like a judge presiding over his courtroom.

Whenever an animal or group of animals was brought into the corral, the auctioneer started the bidding. A string of words poured from the auctioneer's mouth with such velocity and power that I felt like I was being assaulted by a sixty-mile-per-hour wind: *A fine bunch of feeder cattle; who will give me fifteen cents, fifteen—there's fifteen, now sixteen, anybody sixteen, sixteen, sixteen, now seventeen, seventeen, seventeen, anybody seventeen, there's seventeen, now eighteen, anybody eighteen, eighteen, now eighteen, eighteen, anybody eighteen, there's eighteen, now nineteen, anybody, nineteen, nineteen, nineteen, there's nineteen, now twenty, anybody twenty, twenty—nineteen to…*and he pointed to the buyer who had just purchased the feeder cattle for nineteen cents a pound.

As he spoke, the auctioneer looked from face to face in the audience, trying to elicit a nod from potential buyers. All I saw and heard was the auctioneer with his constant barrage of words, his eager eyes searching the audience, his one hand pointing toward buyers, and the other clutching his authoritative gavel. Suddenly the barrage of numbers stopped, the gavel landed with a heavy "bang!" on the counter, and we were ready for the next group of animals to be sold. Somehow through all of this noise the business at hand was handled with great efficiency, but it was definitely more than a little boy could follow.

After our pigs were sold, and, if they were feeder pigs, they were unloaded into the buyer's truck, we were free to go. But then, if I was lucky, Dad asked: "Would you like some ice cream?"

"Sure!"

So we went to the lunchroom, where Dad had a piece of pie and a cup of coffee while I enjoyed my dish of ice cream. Plus, the farmers had a chance to share the latest farming news.

Dad frequently asked Art Van Dam, an older gentleman who lived across the road from us, to ride along to Hopkins as well. When he did we always had to stop in Monterey Center on the way home. Monterey Center was so small that if you blinked with just one eye you might miss it. This was possible because the only building in Monterey Center I can remember was one tiny gas station. But this little station carried the brand of cigar that Art Van Dam preferred, so we always stopped there.

Trips to the livestock auction soon became a thing of the past, however. Dad continued to enjoy his farming, but it was becoming increasingly obvious that he was no longer able to make a living for his family on his eighty-acre farm with the buildings he had. For the past few years he had farmed some of Grandpa's and Alice Van Dam's farms and housed additional chickens in their chicken coops. But it still wasn't enough. Dad had to make a difficult decision.

There were two options Dad considered. He could make a major investment into a new building that would enable him to significantly expand his farming operation. The best possibility was a large farrowing coop that would enable him to raise many more pigs. Or he could get a full-time job at something other than farming and scale back to a smaller, part-time operation. When Uncle Ken told Dad he could get him a job at the General Electric factory in Holland, Dad decided to take him up on the offer. In 1962, when I was eleven years old, Dad started work at General Electric.

CHAPTER 7

THE CO-OP

TRACTORS WERE ALWAYS a big part of life on the farm, and I eagerly looked forward to the time when I would be able to drive one myself. As I grew a little older, my pretensions about driving a real tractor became stronger. One of my favorite activities was sitting on the seat of an idle tractor parked under a shade tree and pretending I was driving it. I turned the steering wheel and pushed various buttons as though I was really in control of the powerful machine on which I sat. Once while doing this, I pushed the starter button on an old tractor hard enough to actually turn the engine over. Suddenly I was terrified, fearing that the tractor might really start moving: what would I do then? That was the end of my tractor play for that day.

Sometimes I rode along with Dad while he was driving tractor. Our tractors had large fenders around the back wheels that I could either lean against or sit on. This provided an ideal place for me to be close to Dad and close to the actions of actual driving. Once, when I was sitting right on Dad's lap on the tractor seat, he allowed me to steer the tractor as we drove it into the garage. That was a very proud day in my young life!

One spring day my opportunity to drive a tractor by myself finally came. Dad was plowing a field to prepare it for planting corn, and he started me disking that same field after he had finished plowing most of it. Dad put me on the seat of our 28-horsepower Co-op, an old-style tractor with tricycle wheels on the front (two wheels close together so that it resembled a tricycle). He showed me how to use the clutch, brakes, shift, and throttle. Then it was time for me to take over. Maneuvering this tractor with the disk behind it over the rough terrain of a plowed field was no easy task. Occasionally the front wheels would hit a large clump of hard clay ground with so much force that they would spin to one side and jerk the steering wheel right out of my hands. This was enough to shake the confidence of a first-time tractor driver to his core. But somehow the Co-op, the disk, and I all survived that experience intact.

Disking a newly plowed field was always a rather challenging experience, especially with the old Co-op. I was afraid of getting stuck in one of the deep furrows left by the plow, so I often left a narrow piece of ground that the disk didn't quite reach along the furrow. Tricycle tractor wheels with no power steering and a disk that was only a little wider than the tractor made disking a difficult job.

Most of my early driving was done on the Co-op, and a lot of Co-op driving meant cultivating corn. Before mounting the cultivators, Dad had to reverse the rear wheels on the Co-op so they would be far enough apart to straddle the two rows of corn being cultivated. I often watched him wrestle the large, heavy, rear wheels of the tractor as he turned them around, tried to keep them balanced so they wouldn't fall, and then re-aligned them so they could be fastened securely back onto the rear axle.

Cultivating was slow, boring work, especially the first time through the corn. Flying across the fields in one of my dreams would have been a lot more fun! The corn was small, and we had shields that protected it from the dirt thrown up by the cultivators. These shields were only about eight inches apart, so I had to keep the row of corn between them. I had to remain very alert or I would find myself cultivating out the corn instead of the weeds (not that that ever happened to me!). We always cultivated the corn twice. The second time it was big enough so that we didn't need the shields. That meant I had a larger margin for error and could go a lot faster. The second time of cultivating was thus a lot easier and more enjoyable than the first.

One of the joys of doing field work with a tractor was the feeling of being a part of the earth and the crops it produced, part of something as natural as the seasons and as big as the planet itself. When we plowed and worked the soil in the springtime, we smelled the warm moisture of the earth's womb as it waited to receive and nourish the soon-to-be-planted impregnating seed. Then there was the delight of watching the rapidly growing crops. And finally there was the joy of reaping a bountiful harvest in the summer and the fall. Driving a tractor in the fields that produced these crops made us a part of this natural, life-giving process.

CHAPTER 8

A NATURAL LIFE

LIVING ON A farm knit us in a powerful way to the natural world and the changing of the seasons. In spring we rejoiced with the coming of the first warm days and the bright sunshine. It was great to see the grass turn green and the trees produce their leaves for another season. A new year of growth was always a time for new hope. Maybe this summer we would get just the right amount of sunshine and rain. Maybe this year we would have a bumper crop of corn.

We had a couple of wooded areas near our farm in which we regularly took walks in the spring and summer. Taking a walk was the perfect Sunday afternoon activity, and the first walk in the spring was a special delight. We scoured the woods and hillsides for the first spring flowers. Adder tongues were usually the earliest to blossom. A little later we found spring beauties, umbrellas, violets, white lilies, and buttercups. Returning home with a freshly-picked bouquet of wildflowers was the perfect culmination of a spring walk.

For Dad, spring meant a busy time of preparing the land for planting corn and oats. Sometimes springtime was so wet that he had to wait before he could safely get onto the field with his tractor and other equipment, and sometimes it was so dry that there was not enough moisture for the crop to come up after it was planted. Oats were usually planted in April and corn in May. What we always hoped for was fairly dry weather while we were working up the soil, followed by a good rain right after the crop was planted. But it didn't usually work out that way.

Summertime, of course, meant that we were out of school. What more did a child need to make any season special? We always had a picnic on the last day of school, including a bonfire and a hotdog roast. I remember one of those picnics where I ate so many hotdogs I felt downright sick as I pedaled my bike home. But I really had to eat that last hotdog. I could never have let my friends eat one more than I did!

Summertime was a lazy time of the year, with lots of opportunities to sleep in and to lie around under a shade tree during a hot afternoon. When it got exceptionally hot, we remarked that it was so hot you could fry an egg on the sidewalk, which would have been hard to do in a community that had virtually no sidewalks! To find relief from the heat, we hauled out the old swimming pool, blew its sides full of air, and filled it with water. What better way to cool off on a hot summer day?

Summers were not all fun and games, however. There were also strawberries to pick, grass to be mowed, corn to cultivate, and times when crops had to be harvested. There was always a concern for enough rainfall during the summer season to keep the corn growing well. When the weather was hot and dry for long periods of time, our church sometimes held a special prayer service for rain. It was always exciting to watch the corn grow from the small seedlings that popped out of the ground in May or June to the hopefully "knee high by the Fourth of July," to the leaves towering over even my Dad's six-foot-three-inches in August, to the mature stalk with two golden ears of corn ready for harvest in October.

By the time September arrived, I was eager for school to start again. Having little to do became old after awhile. And the beginning of a new school year always held a special appeal for me. It was a clean slate with which I could begin: hopefully this school year would be the best one yet!

At home, autumn was special because we watched together the conclusion of another year of growth. The green leaves and stalks of the corn slowly turned brown as the ears grew heavy, felt limp alongside the stalks, and became hard and dry as they awaited their harvest. Pumpkins ripened to a bright orange, and the potato vines died off as they offered their mature fruit hidden in the garden's cooling soil. But the most dramatic presentation of a Michigan autumn was the display put on by her maples and ashes and birches as the green color of spring and summer drained from their leaves to reveal a stunning array of yellow, orange, and red. There are few sights more beautiful than a clear, crisp autumn day in which the frequently cloudy Michigan sky allows the sun to shine without interference for an entire day as it imparts its magical glow to the bright colors of Michigan's trees.

But we could not enjoy such beauty for long. Soon, a day of rain and wind came that swept the leaves from the trees and left them standing barren against the cold, dark skies of November. Soon, the standing stalks of corn were all stripped and flattened by the passing picker and the golden ears were deposited in the corncrib. Soon, the earth was stripped bare, awaiting the first snowfall to give it a winter coat once again.

The first snowfall was always a delight to behold. The beauty of the fresh, white snowflakes quietly descending to cover the drabness of a landscape stripped bare of its produce and foliage brought sincere joy to a young boy's heart.

There was one December in which the earth had remained dark and barren all month until Christmas Eve. We were attending a Christmas party with Dad's side of the family at Uncle Ernie and Aunt Hilda's house. As we sat inside the house playing a game at the kitchen table, we looked outside and saw the first snowflakes coming down under the yard light. It was perfect, and just in time for Christmas!

Of course, snow brought all kinds of new possibilities for outdoor play. When the snow was wet, we rolled it into large balls and made a snowman. If there was a good layer of snow in the pasture, we went sledding or tobogganing down our favorite hill. When the snow piled up in large drifts, we dug caves into them. There was always something fun to do in the snow.

Winters in my childhood seemed to be more severe than they are now. We usually had snow on the ground from early December until the March thaw. Snow drifts frequently shut down our gravel road, and when it was plowed out we had banks of snow that were often four to six feet high. Dad had a snowplow on one of his tractors to clear our driveway and yard. When I was a little older, I sometimes got to do this job. I always tried to pile the plowed snow as high as I could.

Our long driveway was always a challenge in the winter, because it went up a hill from the road to our yard. It was often difficult to get up this hill from the road. Dad always kept some loose sand or gravel around to sprinkle on the driveway for traction. And he frequently had to pull cars up the driveway or out of the ditch on either side. The trick when approaching the driveway was to have enough speed so that you had good momentum heading up the hill, but not so much that you couldn't make the turn at the bottom.

One winter we received so much snow that Dad could not plow our driveway. We had to hire Mr. Den Besten and his dozer to clear it for us. The banks along the sides were ten to twelve feet high when the dozer was done. Mom took pictures of these banks and sent them away to be developed. But, wouldn't you know it, this particular roll of film got lost in the mail, so we lost our only objective record of this winter storm.

CHAPTER 9

EXCURSIONS

THE WORLD I inhabited was very uniform in its thinking and lifestyle. We didn't have any hippies or Communists or unmarried couples living together in Oakland. Everyone took a bath at least once a week and wore clothes that were clean and neat. Almost everyone went to church at least once on Sunday, and many of us, my family included, always went twice. This uniformity and common commitment to shared values gave us the confidence that we were a moral, Christian community. And we saw ourselves as well-protected from the evil influences in the world and society at large.

Every once in a while, however, there was a serious intrusion of evil into our community. One annual occasion that required us to be especially vigilant against worldly influence was the Allegan County Fair. The Fair came to the city of Allegan every September, and we always looked forward to the games and the rides. One day of every Fair week was designated as *children's day*, when all the rides were offered at a special discount. On that day, Pershing School gave us the afternoon off so we could enjoy the Fair.

There was a lot of innocent fun at the Fair. Just walking the fairgrounds was an adventure in itself. There was noise everywhere: the shrieks of girls riding the roller coaster, music from the Merry-Go-Round, cattle bellowing from their barns, and the blare of the announcer calling the harness race on the racetrack. Smells varied from the hot buttered popcorn from the popcorn wagon to the all-too-familiar stench of animals from the barns. There was the press of thousands of other people trying to find their own way around. And, of course, there were the rides—from the Ferris Wheel that towered above everything else to my favorite: the Scrambler. No trip to the Fair was complete for me without a ride or two on the Scrambler.

But along with all the innocent fun there were plenty of suspicious temptations. The hucksters who had brought their game booths to the Fair were constantly prowling about to convince us to try their game. "Get your teddy bear here! Just pop three balloons. Only fifty cents!" Whether it was popping balloons with a dart, knocking over wooden bottles with a ball, or searching for treasure with a remotely operated crane, we all knew our chances for success were slim to none. There were always rumors going around that some of the games were rigged. All the owners were really after was the cash weighing down our pants' front pockets. Even the owners of the rides looked pretty suspect, certainly not the kind of characters I saw in church on Sunday morning. They usually sported a couple of tattoos and a few days' growth of beard. Plus, they were always missing a tooth or two. All of these characters obviously belonged to a class of people that was morally several rungs below the normal society in which I lived. They offered the pleasures of sin for a fee, and if you were not careful you could lose your soul in the bargain too.

The most suspect part of the Fair, however, was the side shows we could see for another outlay of cash. There were always booths offering a look at some fantastic or perverted freak of nature like a 600-pound woman or a pig with two heads. These exotic exhibitions suggested something diabolical at work, and perhaps because of this I rarely visited those booths. But I was always aware of their presence and their dubious aura. Indeed, it was not difficult to imagine that the devil himself might be lurking somewhere in the shadows of a tent as evening fell on the fairgrounds. Thus we had to exercise a great deal of vigilance as we enjoyed the sights and experiences of the Fair.

But some contacts with a larger world were of an entirely different nature.

It was a Saturday evening. Mom told me to take my bath quickly because Dad had a surprise for us. So I hurried through my bath and put on some clean school clothes. After everyone had finished bathing, Dad announced that we were going to eat out at Russ' Restaurant. What a thrill! We all piled into the car for the thirty-minute ride to Holland, and I kept thinking about the delicious food I was about to enjoy.

Russ' Restaurant consisted of a small building with two wings extended out at right angles to each other. Each of these wings included a long, narrow canopy with a center sidewalk and parking spots for cars on either side. When we arrived, Dad drove past both of the drive-in wings only to discover that all the parking spots were full. So he parked off to the side to wait for an opening.

When our turn came, Dad drove the car into the available spot. A large placard alongside the car displayed the menu. It didn't take me long to decide what I wanted: a cheeseburger, French fries and a chocolate milk. Then for dessert I wanted a chocolate sundae.

When our order had been placed, there was nothing to do but wait impatiently for the food to arrive. I watched with fascination as the waitresses kept appearing with trays of food from the constantly swinging door in the side of the restaurant. It was amazing how so much food could come from such a small building! There was something magical about it all: the double-swinging door at the side of the restaurant that opened just long enough to allow another waitress to emerge, but not enough to see what actually went on inside; the young waitresses dressed in white, emerging like fairies from a magical kingdom; the large, heavy trays of food balanced on their delicate young arms; the steaming hot food carried rapidly through a frigid winter wind.

I watched as several trays of food passed our car to some other lucky family. Finally, one of the waitresses turned into the narrow aisle right next to our car. Our feast had arrived! She placed the tray full of food on a small platform alongside our car and pushed the swivel arm below it toward the car so Mom could easily reach it.

She announced the total for the meal, and Dad dug his billfold out of his back pocket and selected the correct bills to pay the tab. After receiving his change, he and Mom began to distribute the food. We all checked to make sure we had the right stuff. Then Dad offered a brief prayer. Once we heard his "Amen" we were free to dig in.

When everyone had finished eating, we collected the empty cups and wrappers and deposited them all on the tray outside the car. Mom pushed the tray as far back from the car as possible, and Dad slowly backed the car out of its spot. Soon another hungry family would take our place. But by then we were safely on our way home, full and happy to have enjoyed another great meal at Russ' Drive-In Restaurant.

CHAPTER 10

THE SACK RACE

WHILE I WAS in the sixth grade, Pershing School combined with two other small country schools to form Bentheim Elementary School. A new brick building with seven classrooms and a gymnasium was built. When I started the seventh grade, I went to school in this new building at Bentheim, which was part of the larger Hamilton School District.

Bentheim School brought several changes into my school life. For the first time, my younger sister, Gayle, and I rode a bus instead of riding with Mom or Aunt Toni. This meant a longer trip back and forth to school, but it relieved our parents of having to transport us. When I got to school, I found myself in a classroom with fourteen eighth graders and the same eight seventh graders that were part of my grade from Pershing School. Mr. Lampen was still our teacher. In the eighth grade, my following year, there were twenty-three students.

Having a gymnasium made several new activities possible. We started a basketball team called the Bentheim

Beavers that competed against other schools. The eighth-grade team was called the Big Beavers and the seventh-grade team the Little Beavers. Our school was still small enough so that all the boys were members of these teams.

On Friday mornings Mr. Lampen often took our entire class to the gym to sing some popular songs together. One of the eighth-grade girls played the piano situated in one corner of the gym, while Mr. Lampen led us in singing some of his old favorites out of a songbook. I can still see him tapping his right foot as he enthusiastically led us in singing tunes such as "Clementine" and "My Old Kentucky Home."

Another musical activity made possible by our bigger school and gymnasium was the formation of a band. Mr. Ruffner, a music student at Hope College in Holland, formed one band from seventh and eighth graders and a second band from fifth and sixth graders. I chose to play a cornet and joined the older band, which consisted of thirteen members. Our little band learned a lot together and even gave a small concert for the public near the end of the school year.

In May of each year, Bentheim held a track and field day. This was not a competition with other schools, but strictly an event for students at our own school. Mr. Lampen made up a formula based on one's age, height, and weight to divide us into different classes for competition. Even in the eighth grade I weighed so little that I competed in Class B rather than Class A.

One of the events on track and field day was a sack race. Each of us boys in Class B received a large burlap sack. We lined up behind the starting line and got both of our feet into the sack. Once everyone was ready, Mr. Lampen stood at one end of the line to start us off.

"Ready! Set! Go!" And we were off.

I grasped the top of my sack tightly in my right hand and extended my left hand out in front of me to help keep my balance. Jumping forward one long hop at a time, I lurched forward in fits and starts. A few boys lost their balance and fell to the ground. By the time they recovered the rest of us were well ahead of them. There were two or three boys right alongside of me competing for the lead. I grasped my bag more tightly than ever, jumped as hard and as far as I could, and struggled to maintain my balance. The finish line was in sight. The rest of the kids were all yelling and screaming at us. Forgetting everything else, I pushed myself forward until one final jump sent me over the finish line in first place.

Winning the sack race wasn't as exciting as flying, but it was still very important to me. We received blue, red, and white ribbons for first, second, and third place in each class. I received a blue ribbon for the sack race that day, plus red ribbons for the broad jump and one-hundred-yard dash, and a white ribbon for the one-hundred-fifty-yard dash. In the eighth grade I earned a blue ribbon for broad jump and white ribbons for the one-hundred-yard dash and the one-hundred-fifty-yard dash. I still have all of these ribbons today.

CHAPTER 11

FAMILY MATTERS

ONE AFTERNOON WHEN I came home from school, I discovered that Mom had been sick in bed all day. When Bev got home from high school a little later, she started making supper. After awhile, Dad came in from doing chores and helped Bev finish with supper. Then Dad, Bev, Gayle, and I sat down for our meal. Dad offered his usual prayer with an additional request for an improvement in Mom's health. After supper Dad, Bev, and I did the dishes together.

Mom's health was always an up-and-down affair. We never knew from one day to the next how she would be feeling. Dad occasionally had to help her with making meals. The doctors were never able to diagnose exactly what was wrong with Mom. She was hospitalized for depression a couple times and received shock treatments, but any improvement was only temporary. Later, Dr. Yff put her on a new medication for depression that helped her considerably. But then it was taken off the market a few months later, and he never did find a good substitute for it. So Mom continued to struggle.

While Mom struggled with her own health and fulfillment in life, she had high hopes for her children. More than once she told us, "I've always prayed that one of you would be a full-time Kingdom worker." This meant a minister or missionary or possibly a Christian school teacher. Since I was the only boy in the family, I felt a special burden to fulfill this motherly expectation. Women could be missionaries or teachers too, but at that time and place men were still considered the breadwinners and bore the greatest responsibility for fulfilling any expected career role.

Should I try to become a minister? Was this God's calling on my life? I thought a lot about this as I pursued my studies at school. It was true that I was a good student, and I liked the idea of becoming a recognized leader in the community. I wanted to find some way to rise above the small, rural horizons that defined my childhood. But was I ready to take this heavy mantle on my narrow shoulders? Or was I destined for something else?

I didn't have a lot of time to sit around and ponder my future, however. If I wasn't busy studying at school or helping Dad at home on the farm, I was probably gone with my family, visiting others. It seemed like we were always visiting somebody. Grandpa and Grandma lived just a half mile down the road, so we saw them often. Uncle Ken (Mom's brother) and Aunt Toni lived next door. Mom also had a sister in Hamilton and one in Holland, both about a half hour's drive away. So we visited all of them often too.

Dad's family was a lot more complicated. I used to say that Dad's mother had six children, his father had six children, and that all together there were nine. This is how I arrived at my math. Originally there were two couples, Mr. and Mrs. Boerman and Mr. and Mrs. Reinink. Each of these couples had three children. Then Mrs. Boerman and Mr. Reinink died. The two surviving spouses, Mr. Boerman and Mrs. Reinink, were then married and had another three children. Thus there were nine in all, with Dad being the oldest of the last group of three.

The oldest three Boerman children were so much older than Dad that we never got to know them very well. We did, however, occasionally visit Uncle Pete in Decatur, about an hour and a half away. Uncle Pete was a retired farmer whose yard featured a collapsed barn and whose house required care in walking through so as not to trip over the clutter. We knew the Reininks better because they were a little younger and lived closer, but they were still a lot older than our family.

That left Dad's two full siblings, a brother and a sister. We visited with them often. Uncle Gil and Aunt Della would sometimes drop in unannounced on a Saturday night. My cousin Paul was just a few months older than me, and we enjoyed playing together.

On one such evening, my sister Bev and I sat down with our cousins, Paul and Sue, to play a game of Uncle Wiggily. The game started smoothly as we took turns advancing slowly along the pathway to Dr. Possum's office. When Sue's turn came up at one point, however, she accidentally dropped the card that stated her next move. The card fell under Paul's chair and he grabbed it before Sue could. He glanced at what it said, decided he didn't like it, and told Sue she had to pick a different card.

"No, I want that one!"

"You dropped it, so you have to pick a new one."

"That's my card, Paul. Give it back!"

This exchange escalated until Paul and Sue were wrestling each other for possession of the disputed card. Finally, Paul pushed his sister onto the floor. Sue burst into tears and ran into the living room to appeal to a higher power.

Soon Uncle Gil strode into the kitchen. "Paul Alan Boerman! Can't you play a game for ten minutes without getting into a fight? What's the problem here?" He grabbed Paul by the shoulder and swung him around in his chair.

"Sue dropped her card and I told her to pick up another one!"

"You give her that card back right now!"

"Okay."

"And I don't want to hear any more fighting here or I'm taking you outside for a lickin'. Do you understand?"

"Yes."

Uncle Gil returned to the living room, and the rest of the game proceeded without incident. Paul and Sue always got into a fight when we started playing a game together. This was embarrassing to us because my sisters and I rarely fought.

There were also a few families from our church with whom we visited regularly, usually on Sunday night after church. Our parents spent the evening in the living room while we kids usually played a game at the kitchen table.

These family visits were the most frequent activity on our family social calendar. This meant that I spent a lot of time with cousins my age. We played games together, rode our bikes together, and went sledding together in the winter. During the summer we took turns sleeping overnight at each other's houses. I wore hand-me-down shirts from my older cousins, Norm and Paul, and in turn passed them down to Kerry and Danny. Our social network was not very extensive, but what it lacked in extent it more than made up for in intensity.

CHAPTER 12

GIFTS

A COUPLE WEEKS before Christmas, Dad and Mom bought a Christmas tree and Dad set it up in the living room. Mom and my two sisters strung the garland and strings of lights around the tree. Now it was December 24th, the tree was aglow with the bright lights, the bobelaars were bubbling away, and the floor was piled high with carefully wrapped presents. Once the supper dishes were finished, we all assembled in the living room. It was time for the annual opening of our family presents.

There was one small gift marked "Bev, Dan, and Gayle." We let Gayle open this, because she was the youngest. Inside there was only a picture of a toboggan. Dad explained that he and Mom had gotten us a toboggan that was out in the barn, since it was too big to wrap. We had used sleds for a long time, but this was a new toy to try out in the snow. We couldn't wait to try it out. My individual gift from Bev and Gayle was a Hardy Boys novel. Mom made me hold it up and smile while she snapped a picture. Mom opened her gift and found she had received a beautiful yellow sweater that Dad and Bev picked out together. Dad opened his and found an electric drill inside, the first electric drill he had ever owned.

"Is that what you wanted?" Mom asked. "I sent for it from a catalog."

"Well, I really wanted a three-eighth's chuck rather than a quarter. A quarter-inch is pretty small."

I didn't understand why Dad objected to his quarter-inch drill. It seemed like he was just being ungrateful.

That spring Dad had another gift for us. He found a good burlap bag and stuffed it about half full of straw. Then he tied a large rope onto it and we had a bag swing. The straw in the bag formed a large ball on which we could sit if we wrapped our legs around it. Dad hung the swing on a low branch from an old apple tree. After some experimenting we discovered that the best way to get a good ride was to use the stepladder as a launching pad. If I positioned the ladder at the far end of the swing's range, I could hold the bag in my hands while climbing up the ladder and jump onto the bag from there. This gave me enough momentum to enjoy a good swing back and forth. It was almost as much fun as flying!

Sometimes we managed to fit two of us on this swing at the same time, although we didn't jump off the ladder on those occasions. But on one particular day the following summer, Bev and I were swinging together. As we came to the far end of one of our swings, the rope suddenly broke and we went hurtling to the ground on top of each other. We both ran crying to Mom in the house. She doctored us up with our Watkins salve and put some Band-Aids over the worst bruises on our knees and faces. After that, Dad checked the rope on our swing more often to make sure it was safe.

CHAPTER 13

GETTING RICH

IT WAS THE middle of July. Dad had finished combining our wheat, but we still needed to bale the wheat straw to be stored as bedding for the animals. Dad never had a baler of his own, so our neighbor, George Engelsman, baled it for us. Dad first raked the straw into long, narrow rows that were ready for the baler to gulp up and compact into the rectangular bales of straw that we then had to gather up and stack on our hay wagon.

Baling required the participation of two or three capable men who could carry and throw a bale of straw with authority. Usually we had two young men helping us. As I drove our tractor and wagon slowly through the field, these two men picked up the straw bales one at a time and brought them to the wagon, where Dad stacked them neatly so they would ride safely back to the barn. When the wagon was almost full, the guys picking up the bales had to throw them up several feet onto two or three layers of bales. I couldn't wait until I was big and strong enough to do this myself.

When we arrived back home with our load of straw, Dad drove the tractor and wagon as close as possible to the barn and the waiting elevator. Just as the tractor neared the barn, he turned sharply off to the side. Someone put a block of wood behind a wagon wheel, and I unhooked the wagon from the tractor. Then Dad swung the tractor around behind the wagon and pushed it until it was right up to the barn. Now it was situated right alongside the elevator so we could unload the bales easily onto the elevator.

Baling straw was one of the rites of summer passage on the farm. It was always hot and hard work. Straw was ready for baling in July, the hottest month of the year, and it had to be done in the afternoon, the hottest time of the day. Early in the morning the straw was still too damp to be baled. But there was still something exciting and celebratory about the whole process, because it represented bringing in the harvest and the muscular exercise of being an active farmer. When I got a little older, I was glad to prove my masculinity by throwing straw bales around with as much dispatch as Dad's hired men used to do.

One winter we heard the news that the Bentheim pickle factory, just a few miles away, was going to offer a new service. During the pickle season they would have a truck that went around twice a week to pick up pickles from small growers. This sounded like a great opportunity for us. All we had to do was grow and pick the pickles, and a truck would come right to our farm and pick them up! How much easier could making money get? Immediately I had visions of my bank account growing by several hundred dollars each summer.

In the spring, Dad plowed and tilled the field next to the house and kept part of it for our pickle patch. He marked off the rows with the corn planter, and then we walked down the rows planting our seed. Once the pickles came up we had to hoe and weed them. We watched with great anticipation as the plants grew and blossomed and started producing small pickles. Soon we could begin picking, and the money would start rolling in!

The first picking went pretty fast, because there weren't many pickles on yet. It didn't take long, but we only filled half of a burlap bag. The next picking was a different story. By the time I got out of bed and had breakfast, the morning sun was already high in the sky and it was hot. I grabbed my pail and walked to the end of a row. I got down on my knees and started combing the vines to look for pickles. Both the vines and the pickles themselves are pretty prickly, so my hands soon felt irritated and itchy. The sun kept getting hotter and hotter, and the sweat started pouring down my face. An obnoxious fly kept buzzing around my head.

After what seemed like several hours, I finally got up off my knees and sat on the edge of my pail. In spite of all my hard work, my pail was only half full. Then I glanced up and down my row: I had finished only a fraction of this row! And this was only the first row! Now I began to see this scheme of pickle raising for what it really was: an evil plot to torture innocent young children. After all, why else would an adult enter into a contract with children to grow pickles? Pickles were the most disgusting thing I ever sank my teeth into. They were dirty and smelly and tasted like something the dog picked up off the road. I couldn't imagine anyone really enjoying them. Any adult who could actually enjoy eating these disgusting things had to be a bit cruel and sadistic.

At any rate, picking pickles turned out to be one of the great trials of my early life. After the first couple times the excitement died quickly. My older sister, Bev, had a lot more persistence at this job than I did, but my younger sister, Gayle, and I always struggled to endure another picking.

Sometimes Dad or Mom had to help us finish picking in order to get the job done. This made me feel guilty, but I still had a hard time motivating myself. When we were done, we usually had two or three burlap bags full of pickles. We set these out for the truck and attached the individual tags which identified them as ours. When they got to the factory the pickles were graded by size. This grading was another part of the exploitative nature of this business. The small pickles, which weighed very little, received a very high price per pound. The large pickles, which weighed a lot, received a low price. So you couldn't win either way. The system was rigged!

The summer I graduated from high school I worked at the same pickle factory in Bentheim that had contracted to buy the pickles we raised in years past. This factory had huge outdoor vats that held brine and pickles for a period of time until the pickles were ready to be canned and marketed. On a few occasions I observed some of the regular male employees relieving themselves directly into these vats. Apparently their opinion of pickles was not too different than mine!

CHAPTER 14

THE RIDE OF MY LIFE

FULL OF ENERGY and anticipation, I stood on top of the hill grasping my sled in my hands, ready to start down the hill on another adventure. The pasture was blanketed with a thick layer of snow, punctuated by a few large weeds and the fence posts that marked its boundary. A cool winter breeze tickled my face as my boots crunched the packed snow beneath the feet that were about to launch me on my next downhill ride. And always there was the hope that the next ride would be the fastest and farthest of all. The confidence I felt as I grasped my sled in my hands and the excitement of another ride down the hill were the perfect recipe for joy.

Suddenly, I plunged forward with all the energy my eager frame could muster and I was off down the hill, the steel runners of the sled gliding smoothly over the well-worn track I had made, the cold air assaulting my determined face, and the snowy hillside flying past in my peripheral vision like tall weeds along the side of a country road. How fast, how far would I go this time? Finally, as the sled gradually slowed and eventually stopped in the gully at the bottom, there was the satisfaction of another successful run down the hill.

The snow of a Michigan winter provided many opportunities for childhood fun, but downhill sledding was my favorite. We were fortunate to have some large hills in our cow pasture not far from the house, and the pasture always had a grassy surface under the snow that was ideal for sledding. Some sliding hills had trees or other obstacles we had to avoid. Others had a fence line near the bottom, and we were always in danger of ending up with a bent-up sled and a gash on our forehead if we travelled too far. And some hills were simply too short or flat to be interesting. But our favorite hill was just right: it was free of obstacles and long and steep enough to give a good ride. Plus, it had a large, open area at the bottom that allowed us to keep going quite a distance when the sledding was good.

The sleds we used then—the only kind we knew—were wooden sleds with steel runners. When we began sledding, the runners cut through the loose snow and made a track a few inches deep. We wouldn't go very fast or very far at first because there was too much resistance. But if we kept following the same path, eventually we established a good track and kept going faster and farther each time. Of course, there were always the times when we got off track and plowed straight into a big drift of loose snow. But with some care and practice we were usually able to stay on the track we had started.

The only respectable way to sled was the belly flop. This meant I laid my belly on the sled, held my head up to see where I was going, and held my hands on the handles at either side to steer. Once I had some experience with the belly flop, I could make a fast running start, jump on the sled as I ran, and head down the hill with lots of momentum.

There were a couple hazards to the belly flop, though. If I got stopped suddenly it was easy to slide off the front of the sled and get my face full of snow. Or I might even get wet, since our hill ended in a gully that sometimes had open water concealed under the snow. And then there was the time the nails that held the boards of my old sled together started to come loose. When I came to one of my abrupt endings, I slid forward and found that a loose nail had ripped a big hole in the front of my coat. But, hey, how could I have any fun if I never took a risk? Sitting upright on a sled was like eating chicken without using my fingers.

One of the challenges my two sisters and I faced was that we had only two sleds between the three of us. There was one smaller, older sled that was okay except that it was so stiff we could hardly steer it. Then there was the newer, slightly larger one that steered well and was my personal favorite. I usually tried to get Bev to use the older sled since she was the biggest. But if Gayle was along, we had to do some sharing. Sometimes we took turns. At other times the two of us went together on one sled. When Gayle was small, this could mean having to endure the boredom of sitting up on the sled behind each other. Or sometimes we did a double deck belly flop, one on top of the other. Yes, this did work! The biggest disadvantage was that you couldn't make a running start. You simply had to pile on top of each other, give yourself a little push, and go from there. Also, if you weren't careful, a sharp turn partway down the hill could send the top person sprawling into the snow. This sometimes worked well to get rid of a younger rider you really didn't want along, anyway—not that I ever used it for that purpose!

When we got a little older, our parents bought us a toboggan. This offered a new variation on downhill sledding; all three of us could ride down the hill together.

But a toboggan required a steeper hill than did our sleds, so we experimented sliding down different hills. Although we enjoyed using the toboggan, for me there was nothing quite like the old, single, belly flop on the sled.

During the winter of 1963, when I turned twelve years old, we had a slight thaw followed by an ice storm. Since there was already a good layer of snow on the ground, the ice accumulated on top and formed a smooth, icy covering over everything. I don't remember how thick the ice was, but I know it was thick enough to support us kids walking on it. This enabled us to roam the winter world freely without having to trudge through the snow; we could walk right over top of it. The only problem was staying upright; that ice sure was slippery!

As Bev and I explored this new icy wonderland one day, we began to wonder where we could go for a sled ride on top of this ice. We didn't dare go down our regular hill for two reasons: we were afraid we would go too far and run into the barbed-wire cow fence; we were also sure we would never be able to get back up the hill again. But certainly there had to be someplace we could sled, and sled on a scale we had only dreamed of before.

As we surveyed our farm, we saw there was a gentle slope all the way across from west to east. So, if we stood at the west end of the farm, we would be looking downhill all the way to the east end. Ordinarily these hills were not steep enough for sledding, but this was not an ordinary winter day. So we set out, walking, slipping, falling, and sliding our way to the west end of our farm, pulling our sleds along.

Finally, we made it to the high end of the farm. It was a beautiful sight! As we looked to the east, all we could see was a gently sloping sheet of ice practically begging for a sled to fly across it. We looked at each other with some hesitation and then agreed to try it together. Simultaneously we draped our sled ropes over the top of the sleds, grasped them firmly by the sides, gave the best push-off we could without slipping, and we were off.

The prospect was exhilarating. All we could see before us was glittering ice and snow. The sleds accelerated quickly as they glided effortlessly over the smooth ice. We had never before experienced such a quick, easy slide. Usually we wished we could push ourselves to make our sleds go faster. But not this time. We kept going faster without moving a muscle. The crystals of ice started flying past at an incredible rate of speed. No longer aware of where my sister and her sled were, all I could see was raw ice whizzing by ten inches under my chin at a rate of speed I never imagined I would experience on a sled. It felt a bit like flying!

My heart rate began to accelerate as rapidly as my sled. My thoughts quickly turned from achieving a fast start to wondering how I could slow down my runaway sled. I didn't dare to try turning to slow it down, because I was afraid the momentum would send me sprawling out onto the ice. What else could I do? My mind went blank. My hands on the wooden crosspiece that steered the sled were frozen in place. And still the sled kept going faster. There was nothing I could do but hang on desperately, hoping that somehow I could survive this ride of terror I could not escape. But where would it end?

Then, as I looked ahead, I saw it: the road! Never imagining my ride would take me this far, it was now obvious that I would soon hit the road. This presented two awful possibilities. There was a deep ditch along this road. If we fell into the ditch we would be plastered against its side like tomatoes hurled against a cement wall. There could also have been a large bank of snow along the road, standing in our way. In that case, the momentum of our ride would drive us headfirst into the snow bank like sixteen-penny nails driven halfway into a two-by-four. But fortunately, conditions were just right. There was no tall snow bank, and the ditch was drifted over with snow and ice so that we could cross over safely. The surface was smooth and level.

But what if there was a car coming? Glancing quickly in both directions, I was relieved to see nothing. Gasping a quick prayer for safety, I flew straight forward over the road and into the field on the other side. Bev and I continued for some distance into this field before the ground leveled enough to finally bring our sleds to a halt.

My heart was still beating about five hundred times a minute, but at least I knew we were safe. I don't know how fast we actually went on our sleds that day, but it was definitely faster than I ever wanted to go again. We waited for the ice to thaw before we went sledding again that winter.

CHAPTER 15

THE FATEFUL JUMP

DAD AND I were on the way to Hamilton to get our haircuts. He told me he would drop me off at the barbershop while he stopped at the hardware store and the bank.

"I should be back by the time you're finished with your haircut."

"Okay."

Dad pulled his pickup in front of the barbershop, and I jumped out and walked into the shop. There was one customer in the chair when I walked in, but no one else was waiting. Soon, the barber was done with him and it was my turn.

"Ready for your haircut, young man?"

"Yup," I said as I got up and walked to the chair.

Then I sat quietly as the barber carefully trimmed my wavy red hair down to a more manageable length. I waited impatiently for Dad to appear through the front door. The door opened once, but an unfamiliar man and his son came in and took their seats to wait their turn. What was taking Dad so long? He said he would be back before I was done.

Soon, the barber was finished. He brushed away the loose hair from my neck and removed the white cape that kept the cut hair from collecting on my clothes.

"Think your mother will be happy with that?" the barber asked.

"Yuh, I think so," I muttered as I tried to figure out what to do next. Dad had still not appeared, I didn't have any money to pay the barber, and I didn't want to stay in the barbershop waiting for him. So I did the only thing I could think of: I walked out without paying and without offering a word of explanation. The barber made no attempt to stop me as I left.

Once outside in the bright sunshine, I squinted and scanned the horizon for Dad's green Chevy pickup. Sure enough, there it was at the bank just a little ways down the street. I hurried down the street and arrived at the truck just as Dad emerged from the bank.

"All done already?"

"Yup!"

"You beat me!"

"I know. I only had to wait a few minutes."

Then Dad drove his pickup back to the barbershop and we entered it together. Dad had to wait his turn to get his haircut, and when he was finished he paid for both of our haircuts. Now my conscience was finally clear.

At another visit to this same barbershop, I was getting my haircut and Dad was waiting for his turn. The barber started talking to another customer who was still waiting, also.

"Did you hear what Norm Poll did?"

Dad and I instantly perked up, because Norm was my cousin and Dad's nephew. The Poll family lived in Hamilton.

The barber continued. "He came home with a trophy from Martin U.S. 131 Dragway last week, and Earl (Earl was Norm's dad and my uncle) didn't even know he had gone there."

Dad and I exchanged a grin, but neither of us said anything.

"I guess Norm had a little explaining to do after that!" laughed the customer.

"Yeah, I don't think Earl was too happy about that."

My cousin Norm was known for having one of the fastest cars around. His 283 horsepower 1961 black Chevrolet could beat almost anyone in the quarter mile. Norm was also known for pushing his limits. But coming home with a trophy from a race his parents didn't even know he was part of might have pushed his limits a little too far. Dad and I had a good chuckle about that as we drove home.

During the following summer I stayed overnight with Norm and his sister, Kathy. One night Aunt Juella took the three of us to a small lake to go swimming. For me this meant simply splashing around in the water because I had never learned how to swim. I watched with envy as Norm dove off a diving board into water eight or ten feet deep, emerged shortly afterward, and swam back to the diving platform. Aunt Juella had a large inner tube along, and for some time I floated around contentedly on this tube. But after awhile I decided it was time for a change of pace.

Aunt Juella was standing several feet away in the water. I slid off the side of the inner tube only to find that I was in water that was as deep as I was tall! Sputtering and gasping for air, I moved desperately toward shore until I reached water that was shallow enough so that I could breathe freely. I hadn't realized how deep the water was.

Aunt Juella laughed. "You didn't have to worry. I was only a few feet away!"

But for me it was no laughing matter. Jumping into water over my head was a terrifying experience. I've been afraid of water ever since.

In addition to staying overnight at my cousins' houses, Grandma usually had me and my cousin Kerry stay overnight once a year with her and Grandpa. When it was time to go to bed at Grandma's house, she led us to a door that opened from the living room to reveal a narrow set of steep wooden steps leading upstairs. We followed her up. At the top of the steps stood Grandma's Victrola record player that had to be cranked by hand. Sometimes she let us play one of her old records on it.

Grandma led us past the record player into the spare bedroom. The bedroom was sparsely furnished with only a double bed and a chest of drawers. The faded window shade with tears along the edges and the delicate lace curtains looked so fragile that they might shatter with just a touch of our hands. The room smelled like a jar of fruit abandoned for years in the cellar.

The cool, wooden floorboards creaked under our bare feet as we hurried to climb into the bed Grandma had prepared for us. It felt good to slide between the clean sheets and feel their warmth surround us.

Once we were settled comfortably in bed, Grandma went out into the hallway and got something out of the closet. She returned with a large metal pot. The pot had a wire handle for carrying, three small, pointed feet for resting on the floor, and a heavy metal lid.

Setting the pot on our bedroom floor a little ways from the bed, Grandma said, "You can use this if you have to go to the bathroom during the night."

"Okay. Thanks, Grandma."

"Good night, boys!"

"Good night, Grandma."

"I'll leave the hall light on so you can see."

"Okay."

Kerry and I slept through the whole night without any need to relieve ourselves in Grandma's specially positioned pot. But when we got up in the morning and saw that pot still standing there, we knew we had to try it out simply for the novelty of the experience. So Grandma had to empty and clean her chamber pot solely as a result of our curiosity.

CHAPTER 16

MOVING ON

THE FALL OF 1964 featured the presidential election between President Lyndon Johnson and Senator Barry Goldwater. Seeking to inspire our interest in the political process, our teacher, Mr. Lampen, set up a debate to argue the merits of the two candidates and their vice-presidential running mates. I volunteered to be a debater and was assigned to make a two-minute speech in favor of Hubert Humphrey as Johnson's running mate. This required some research into his life. On the basis of my study, I argued that Mr. Humphrey's experience as mayor of Minneapolis and his career in the U.S. Senate made him a very qualified candidate for Vice President. I don't remember who won that debate, but I enjoyed being part of the process.

In the spring of 1965, when I was fourteen, I sat at my desk gazing out at the Bentheim School playground. This playground had been host to both my glory and my shame: kicking a goal for my soccer team, striking out again at home plate, making a surprisingly good catch in right field, and getting kicked in the shins when a classmate missed the soccer ball and hit me instead. Then my eyes drifted inside to the familiar classroom in which I sat: Mr. Lampen explaining an arithmetic problem to the seventh graders; my classmate Linda looking as pretty and unapproachable as ever; and the report card I would soon receive for the last time filled once again with all A's and B's. Soon all this familiarity would be gone. Soon my grade school days would be over.

Then it happened. The day of my eighth-grade graduation came. The twenty-one students in our graduating class filed into the front two rows of our Oakland Christian Reformed Church. We listened to the commencement address given by the minister of the Bentheim Reformed Church.

Next came the high point of the ceremony for me. I was probably the poorest softball player of all the boys in the eighth grade, and my abilities on the basketball court weren't much better. I was so quiet that I had a difficult time making friends. But I could study and learn well, and I played my cornet pretty well in our band. I felt rewarded and vindicated when Mr. Lampen chose my classmate Bob Hoffman and me to play a cornet duet for our graduation. We played the well-know hymn "Abide with Me." Mom remarked to me afterward that she thought this hymn was a rather sad song to play at a commencement ceremony, but for me it was simply a symbol of my triumph in graduating with distinction from grade school. I had finished elementary school and was ready to move on to a bigger and better world. I was flapping my wings and looking forward to a new kind of flying.

FLIGHT SCHOOL 301

CHAPTER 1

THE HIGH SCHOOL GYM CLASS

STARTING HIGH SCHOOL meant entering a whole new world. My parents wanted me to go to a Christian high school, so I was enrolled at Holland Christian High School. My day started with a forty-minute bus ride. The bus carried grade school through high school students from our church and community to the Christian grade schools and high school in Holland. Seating on the bus was generally in a hierarchical order, with the youngest children in front and the older students in the back. Merle and Billy, the two senior boys, reserved the two back seats for themselves. These seats were such exclusive territory that I was once forced to stand up when there were no other seats available. I was standing with one arm clutching a stack of books and the other one holding my cornet case. When our bus made one of its frequent, sudden stops I fell forward, and my books and cornet landed in the center aisle around my fallen body. At that point, Billy felt sorry for me and let me sit alongside him in the back seat.

In Bentheim School I had been part of a class of twenty-one students and a school that had about one hundred forty students in all. All of those one hundred forty students lived in the same rural area in which I had my home. But at Holland Christian I found myself part of a freshman class of two hundred seventeen students, with a total student body of over eight hundred. My freshman class alone was much larger than the entire student body at Bentheim School. And many of the students were residents of the city of Holland who had no understanding of life on a farm.

Although there were four other freshman students whom I knew from our church, they were not in any of my classes. Thus, I did not know one single student in any of my classes that first semester in high school. Getting acquainted and making friends was a huge uphill battle for me. As long as I was busy going to classes I stayed occupied without any problem, but lunch hours were often very lonely. Sometimes I wandered the halls alone, and sometimes I found one or two other lonely guys with whom I could spend my time. But I did not develop many meaningful friendships.

A few times during my freshman year someone stole the sack lunch I had deposited in my locker, so I walked a few blocks to a donut shop and filled up with some fresh pastries. I never found out who did this, but I felt like someone was deliberately singling me out for this unfair treatment.

There were three separate buildings that constituted Holland Christian High School. The original school building consisted of a basement gymnasium and two stories of classrooms above it. Later, another two-story classroom building was constructed across the street. We often had to cross the street to get from one class to another. Then there was the butler building, a small metal building tucked in at the end of the newer classroom building when someone apparently realized they had no place for the school band to practice. So every morning I brought my cornet to the butler building, where it would be ready for me when band hour came up later in the day.

Another part of my high school challenge was the pile of homework I was assigned. In grade school I never had any assignments that I could not complete during school hours. The only time I ever took a book home was to study for a test. Now I received a significant assignment in every one of my classes almost every day, with usually just one short study hall during school hours. I was lucky if I could complete one assignment during study hall. Everything else had to be done at home that night. So I dutifully carried my pile of books home every night and often studied at the kitchen table until 10:00 or 11:00 P.M. Although I enjoyed the subjects I was studying, the sudden change from no homework to three or four hours every night was hard to handle. It took me awhile before I was comfortable with this new workload.

Playing my cornet in band was also a new experience. I had started playing in the seventh grade, but I found out that all the students at Holland Christian had started playing their instruments in fifth grade. This put me two years behind everybody else. Consequently, our band director, Mr. Vander Linde, put me in the junior high band instead of the high school one. I continued to take private lessons with my grade school band director that freshman year to try to catch up with my classmates. I also moved from a band of thirteen members to one with over a hundred.

In the spring, all the bands in the Holland area transformed themselves into marching bands in order to participate in Tulip Time, a festival that celebrates Holland's Dutch heritage. So I had to learn how to march in step with the rest of the band. The hardest part of this was learning to play my cornet and march at the same time. It was like trying to drink a glass of water while riding the pony at the department store. At first I tried desperately to keep my head rigid while my body was moving, but that was impossible. I had to learn to sway my head along with the rest of my body, to develop a natural rhythm of movement that I could maintain while I marched. Soon, marching and playing became easy and natural, and I found that I actually enjoyed it.

Participation in physical education was also a new experience. In grade school we played softball, soccer, and tag during our lunch hours, but we never had an organized gym class. Now I was required to purchase and wear a special set of clothes designed just for physical education. First there was some new-fangled type of underwear that was supposed to offer increased protection during a physical workout. It looked to me like it was designed more to expose than to protect, but I put it on anyway. Then there was a tee shirt and a pair of shorts. Other than swimming trunks and basketball shorts, I had never worn shorts before. Shorts were for women and little kids. No serious man ever wore shorts. But there I was in my newly purchased shorts, with my legs like two white strings of spaghetti exposed for everyone to see.

Once we were all in the gym, our teacher, Mr. Vander Hill, lined us up to do calisthenics. Mr. Vander Hill was built like a Sherman tank. He looked like he could have done a hundred push-ups without even breaking into a sweat. As I looked down the row of my classmates, I saw arms and legs that also looked much more tanned and muscular than mine. But then, as if to emphasize that my skeletal white appearance was not enough to make me stand out, we started to participate in drills and exercises I had never attempted before. The boys next to me seemed to know what was going on, but I was always a step behind: up when I should have been down, down when I should have been up, and generally looking like a soldier out of step with the rest of his company.

Then, at the end of our class, came the worst part of all: we had to strip and take a shower in one large room, where everyone could see everyone else. I removed my clothes with great trepidation and walked squeamishly into the shower room where I briefly rinsed off my sweaty body. Then I hurried back to wrap myself in my towel and head to the locker room where I could re-clothe and become presentable again. This was a whole different experience than sitting in the bathtub at home with the bathroom all to myself. Plus, we had only a few minutes to undress, shower, re-dress, and then get back to our next class before the buzzer rang. Those showers in gym class were the shortest showers I ever took.

All of these new experiences were somewhat overwhelming at first, but I learned to cope and become comfortable with them after awhile. One part of being in school was the same as it had always been: I had to study and learn new things. This I knew I could do, and so I resolved to do it well. I became obsessed with maintaining good grades and managed successfully to earn all A's and B's except for the C's I sometimes got in physical education. These grades meant that I was on the honor roll, a distinction I very much cherished.

In my sophomore year my class was required to take a one-year course in biology. After taking one of the tests in this class, our teacher, Mr. Wyma, informed me that I had the highest test score out of more than two hundred sophomores in our school. Maybe high school wasn't so bad after all! Maybe I could find a way to fly here, too.

CHAPTER 2

AN INSECURE WORLD

WHILE GETTING USED to high school challenged my social and intellectual skills, being part of a larger social scene also made me more aware of the nation and world in which I lived. The sturdy Christian values of my rural environment taught me that it was my Christian duty to oppose Communism as the great, godless evil in the world, and to support Republican politics in our country.

My political assumptions were challenged already several years previously when John F. Kennedy ran for President. Not only was Kennedy a Democrat, he was also a Catholic. This combination formed a double threat to our Protestant Republican values, and I feared that a Kennedy presidency might bring real persecution to us Protestant Republicans. Not much changed, however, when Kennedy was elected, and so those fears subsided. The Cuban missile crisis of 1962 and Kennedy's assassination in 1963 transformed Kennedy into a hero and a martyr. Anyone who stood up to Krushchev and Communism like Kennedy did could certainly not be all bad. And, along with the rest of our nation, I felt genuine remorse at Kennedy's untimely death.

The threat of Soviet Communism continued unabated during my high school years. A nuclear war with Russia seemed like a real possibility. We took a physical education class in high school that taught us about nuclear radiation: how it affects the body, how to recognize its symptoms, and how to treat it. Several public buildings in Holland and other cities were designated as approved nuclear fallout shelters because their construction made them more impervious to nuclear radiation. Many families constructed private bomb shelters to which they could safely retreat in the event of a nuclear war. These shelters were usually a small room dug out of the ground and stocked with enough canned goods to sustain the family for an extended stay.

Life seemed fragile. At any moment some international crisis could escalate into a nuclear exchange that would wipe out our entire civilization as we knew it. But there was always security in the normal routines of the rural life of which I was a part: farming, going to school, attending church, and visiting Grandpa and Grandma or an uncle, aunt, and some cousins.

Even the normal routines of life began to change as I matured, however. Grade school had changed to high school. I was a teenager now, and gradually more adult activities and expectations became the norm.

One of these adult activities for men was pheasant hunting. Pheasants were abundant in those days. We saw them around all the time. I remember one day shortly before pheasant season opened on October 20. As we rode the bus to high school that morning, the boys on the bus counted the rooster pheasants we saw in the fields on our way to school. We counted over one hundred that one morning. And those were just the ones standing out in the open!

Every farm boy was expected to enjoy hunting, so I tried to meet that expectation. Dad bought me a single shot, sixteen-gauge shotgun so I could at least pretend to be a legitimate hunter. October 20, the first day of the season, was like a holiday back then. All of the high school boys from the country skipped school that day to go hunting, even though for us students at Holland Christian that meant having all of our grades docked. I participated in this "illegal" activity as well. The women of the church put on hunters' lunches on October 20. All the hunters in the area came to a designated location for this lunch, and the ladies made a tidy profit for the church.

On the morning of October 20, all the hunters congregated in Uncle Ken's yard next door. Each hunter got out his shotgun and shells, put on his hunter's jacket, and made sure his hunting license was prominently displayed on his back. We had to wait until 10:00 A.M., the official season opening. When 10:00 arrived, we fanned out across the field and began our march through the field to flush out any pheasants that might be hiding there. Most of Uncle Ken's farm had not been worked for a few years and was grown over with tall grass and weeds. This was perfect habitat for pheasants. Sometimes we also went through one of Dad's cornfields, hoping to drive the pheasants out at the end of the long rows of corn.

October 20 was usually a cool, cloudy day. The vegetation in the fields was brown and decaying, lending a pleasantly pungent aroma to the air. Every once in awhile, without warning, as we trudged across the field, the air was suddenly disturbed with the furious beating of a pheasant's wings and the sight of its rapid ascent to escape our threat. If it was a hen, of course, we simply let it go, because it was illegal to shoot them. If it was a rooster, the loud explosions of shotgun shells filled the air in an attempt to bring the bird down. Sometimes the pheasant continued on his course regardless of all the noise, and sometimes he suddenly plummeted until he landed with a thud somewhere up ahead in the long grass.

Although I went pheasant hunting several times, I never once actually killed one. I pretended to be a hunter because it was simply the thing to do, but my heart was never in it. Maybe I would have enjoyed it more if I had been more successful. But killing animals simply never appealed to me. I remember once when Dad was gone for a few days and I had to do the chores for him. There were some sows with small pigs I had to take care of. It was not uncommon for small pigs to get sick and die. Dad told me if any of the little pigs were hopelessly sick, I should put them out of their misery by hitting them over the head with a hammer. I can still recall doing this to one small pig. It was a very hard thing for me to do.

I was never cut out to be a hunter, but in order to fit in I went so far as to skip a day of school in order to hunt. This caused the lowering of all of my grades by one mark. Thus, for example, an A- became a B+ and a B+ became a straight B. I allowed this to happen even though getting good grades in high school was fiercely important to me. My intellectual ability and academic achievement were central to my concept of my own value and dignity as a person. And I was obviously a much better student than I was a hunter! But I still went hunting simply because it was the expected thing for me to do.

Sometimes I went pheasant hunting with Uncle Ken and Uncle Bob on a Saturday or an afternoon after school. On one such occasion, Uncle Ken and Uncle Bob each helped themselves to a can of cold beer after we had returned from our hunt. I was appalled to see my two uncles violate an accepted code of ethics right in front of their sons and nephews. Didn't they know that alcohol was a tool of the devil and strictly forbidden in our community? Events like this caused me serious anxiety. If the values I had been taught as a boy were sometimes violated even by members of my own community, whom could I trust? Where could I find security?

CHAPTER 3

THE SHAVINGS NIGHTMARE

ONE AFTERNOON I arrived home from school and went upstairs into my bedroom to change into my everyday clothes. Then I went out to the pig coop, where Dad had the pickup ready at one end with a ramp and some gates leading up to it. This was Dad's arrangement for loading our fattened pigs, each weighing a little over two hundred pounds, onto his pickup to be taken away for butchering. I found my special plywood board with the handle cut into it that I always used to help drive the pigs.

"Are you ready to go?" asked Dad.

"Yeah, I'm ready."

Dad surveyed the pigs and spotted one of the largest.

"Let's start with that one."

He then walked toward the designated pig to begin separating him from the others and driving him toward the narrow alley made by the gates he had set up. I stood near the entrance to this area to help guide the chosen pig in the right direction.

Once the pig entered this narrow alley, either Dad or I, whoever was closer, closed the area behind him with the board we held and tried to keep him moving in the direction of the pickup.

If a pig was determined to get away, it was hard for me to stop him. An animal that outweighed me almost two to one with a low center of gravity was pitted against a string bean standing behind his piece of plywood. It was like a torpedo hitting a sailboat. I could usually hold the pig back if my feet were firmly in place, but occasionally a determined pig managed to force his way past me or even knock me over, sending me sprawling right into the manure.

Once a pig got away, it was even harder to corner him and drive him onto the pickup on the second try, because he knew there was a way out. But usually Dad and I together managed to get them all loaded. Sometimes Mom or one of my sisters held the pickup tailgate in place to prevent the already-loaded pigs from getting out of the truck bed. Then she lowered it briefly when we were ready to drive the next pig on.

As I grew older, I was able to help Dad with more jobs on the farm. Sometimes I had to fill in on jobs he normally did if he was gone to work. One such job was helping to unload shavings. It was a job I dreaded but knew I had to do.

At about 10:00 on a Saturday morning, a large truck loaded with wood shavings crept up our driveway. Dad had the elevator already set up to carry the shavings into an area of the barn loft reserved for this purpose. We used these shavings as bedding for the sows and their young piglets housed in the west side of the barn. We had a small opening from the loft that allowed us to shove some of the shavings down to the farrowing area where the sows and piglets were housed. There was another small opening in the front of the barn through which the elevator carried the shavings.

Dad was working at General Electric that Saturday, so I had to help unload the shavings. The driver backed his truck up to the elevator. I plugged in the elevator to start it up, and the driver began to unload the shavings into the elevator, which then carried them up to the loft in the barn. My part of this operation was to go into the loft with a fork to keep the shavings leveled off. Otherwise, they would all pile up in one big heap right under the end of the elevator.

Shavings are not very heavy, and the physical demands of keeping the pile leveled off were easily bearable. The hard part was breathing. After the shavings had been coming in for ten or fifteen minutes, the air filled with sawdust so thick that I could barely keep air going in and out of my mouth. Once every few minutes I went to the edge of the enclosed area in the loft, leaned over the side where the air was a little clearer, spit the sawdust out of my throat and caught a couple breaths of fresh air.

Then it was back to the growing pile of shavings again, wading knee deep into the loose pile, squinting to see through the ascending dust, pulling the top of the pile down to a lower spot and panting and gasping to keep enough air in my lungs so I didn't collapse. It was easy to imagine falling into the pile of shavings, suffocating from the dust, and being buried so deep that no one would ever find me. I sure wished I could fly out of that dust-filled room and soar freely in the fresh, crisp air outside! But finally the flow of shavings began to slow, signaling that the load was almost over. As soon as I knew it was safe, I trudged through the heaps of shavings to the ladder, descended, and headed quickly for the clear air outside.

Once outside I removed my glasses and cleaned them off with my handkerchief. I cleared my throat, spit out the contents, and blew my nose so I could finally breathe freely again. Shavings clung to me everywhere. They stuck to my socks and filled my shoes and my pockets. I brushed myself off and congratulated myself on having survived another ordeal. The driver thanked me for my help, picked up his tools, and drove away. Unloading shavings was the most miserable farm job of all.

Fortunately, there were more pleasant jobs. One such job was occasioned by a phone call from Grandma on a Friday night in January. We had a lot of snow that week, and the wind had piled it up into deep drifts scattered all around. Grandma called Mom and asked if I could help Grandpa shovel snow at church the next morning, and Mom told her that would be fine.

At 9:00 on Saturday morning I walked with Dad's large aluminum scoop shovel out to Grandpa's waiting car. Since I was the oldest grandson in the vicinity, it was appropriate for me to give Grandpa a hand with this task. He and Grandma were the custodians at our church. The two of them could handle most of the jobs, but shoveling piles of heavy drifted snow was a difficult job for a seventy-year-old.

When we got to church, Grandpa started shoveling off the sidewalks that went all the way around the building. The snow was not too deep because they were out in the open where the wind blew much of it away. I started clearing the steps of the open entry way on the east end of the church. This was the main entry and it was packed with drifted snow. The west wind blew all the snow toward the east end of the building, then circled around and piled it up in the exposed entry way. Dad's big scoop shovel worked well in digging out the deep drifts of snow that hid the steps from view.

Soon, Grandpa had finished cleaning off the sidewalks, so he and I worked toward each other as I scraped the rest of the snow off the steps and he cleared the area just in front of them. Now people would be free to come up the steps the next morning. Grandpa would throw out some salt early Sunday morning to break up the remaining ice. Our job was done.

As we rode back home, Grandpa told me he wanted to get a shovel just like my Dad's for shoveling snow. He liked how it worked. When he dropped me off, he thanked me for helping him. I brought Dad's shovel back to the garage and returned to the house. It was a good feeling to have helped out Grandpa and to prepare the way for all the people who would come to church the following morning.

CHAPTER 4

THE BASKETBALL GAME

JANUARY 30, 1967, was my sixteenth birthday. Mom picked me up from school in the afternoon and drove me to the Secretary of State Office in Zeeland. There I took a ride with a police officer in the final test to see whether I could acquire my own driver's license. The officer was pretty easy on me, merely requiring me to drive around a few city blocks. Although very tense for this momentous occasion, I apparently maneuvered our family car well enough to satisfy the officer. I had passed my driving test. The coveted license was now mine!

Having my own driver's license opened the door to new possibilities in the social realm, and a new realm of flying for me. Now I could pick up a couple friends and go to the bowling alley in Hudsonville, or to a Sunday evening concert in the Zeeland Bowl, an outdoor stadium used for summer concerts. So I began to share such social outings with a few other guys from my church. This significantly expanded my social horizons.

One social ritual in Holland was the Sunday night driving of Eighth Street. Eighth Street was Holland's main street. After all the churches were done with their evening services, hundreds of teenagers drove their cars back and forth along Eighth Street honking their horns, rolling down their windows, and stopping to talk with each other while holding up all the traffic behind them. This was supposedly a great opportunity to meet girls and get acquainted with other friends, but I never got real excited about it. I participated in this ritual a few times without any spectacular results.

Being able to drive a car also opened up the possibility of taking a girl out on a date, but doing so required overcoming an incredible amount of fear and anxiety. There were certainly plenty of attractive girls in school, but asking one out on a date meant I would actually have to talk to one of them. Not just say "Hi!" or discuss an algebra problem, but actually talk about something interesting. And I would have to initiate this conversation either in person or on the phone with one of those lovely creatures. I could fantasize about such a remote possibility, but I knew it would never happen. Girls were like the basketball trophies that lined the hallway in our high school: something I could admire from a distance but never touch.

The most exciting event on our high school social calendar was the basketball game. There were certainly other sports at Holland Christian High School during the years I attended, but I never watched a single soccer game or track meet, and I did not even know who the team members were. But I still remember many of the basketball players forty years later. Basketball was the one activity that united the school and sent all of us into a state of frenzy. Questioning loyalty to our basketball team in high school would have been as serious a sin as openly advocating for Communism in the political arena. We worshipped our basketball heroes as if they were almost angelic creatures.

One Friday night my friend Jack picked up me and a couple other friends as we made our way to the basketball game that night against Zeeland. We always looked forward to playing Zeeland, because we almost always beat them. In my freshman year, however, we did not have a very good team, and Zeeland beat us in our very first tournament game. They were so thrilled at defeating Holland Christian in a tournament game that they had a glory day to celebrate, and all the students of Zeeland High School paraded through our halls cheering and shouting and disrupting our classes.

But this Friday night was different. We arrived at the Holland Civic Center and joined the other students to fill the lower bleacher section of the building. Adults who attended the games enjoyed their padded seats in the upper deck. After watching our reserves demolish the Zeeland reserves, we looked forward to the varsity game. The noise level in the Civic Center crescendoed as the varsity game began. Our cheerleaders led us in shouting encouragement, and Mr. Vander Linde and the pep band added their rousing music to the cacophony. I'm surprised we never blew the roof off that building with all the noise we made.

Our basketball team in my junior year probably had the tallest front line in the state. Steve Bushouse, our center, was six foot five, and our two forwards, Steve Vogelzang and Dan Brower, were each about six foot eight. We watched as these three giants muscled the ball into the forecourt and consistently shot the ball over the heads of the smaller Zeeland players. Plus, they were an intimidating defensive force that frustrated the Zeeland offensive front line. Soon we were well ahead in the game, and our coach Mr. Tuls began making some substitutions.

Zeeland started out the second half of the game with a full court press, desperate to do something to slow down our momentum. The inbound pass went to Lloyd Dozeman, the guard who usually brought the ball down the court. Lloyd dribbled furiously as he switch-backed across the court to evade the defensive pressure from the Zeeland opponents. We were convinced that if Lloyd were locked up in the county jail and someone managed to smuggle a basketball in to him he would be able to dribble his way out. Lloyd passed the ball to Bob De Nooyer, our other guard, who drained a long shot from the backcourt before anyone could block his shot. We beat Zeeland that night seventy-six to fifty-one.

Our team went undefeated during the course of the regular season that year. We were rated number one in the state. In tournaments we advanced all the way to the state finals. I rode a bus filled with other excited students to the championship game in Lansing that fateful day in March. We were confident of victory. But alas! A guard from Willow Run High School had the best day of his high school career and led his team to upset the previously invincible Holland Christian Maroons. We had to settle for second place.

CHAPTER 5

TAKING MY STAND

SPRINTED UP the brown-painted steps to my upstairs bedroom, then pulled down the window shade to hide the darkness outside. I was too scared to pray, so I scrambled into my pajamas and jumped into bed.

The fear would not go away. I kept seeing Christ returning on the clouds and felt myself desperately digging more deeply under the covers to hide. How could I know that I was really a Christian? How could I be sure I was saved?

I couldn't lie still any longer. Slipping quietly out of bed, I made my way slowly down the steps. As I eased open the door at the bottom, I saw Mom sitting on the couch reading a magazine.

"What's the matter, honey?" Tears were my only response. I sat next to her and she put her arm around me. "Are you worried again about not being saved?" I nodded. Once again she assured me that I was a Christian and had no reason to be afraid.

But how could I be sure? Being a Christian had always been more of an assumption than a conclusion for me.

After all, I was a member of a committed Christian home and church. I attended services faithfully. And I tried hard to be good. I didn't smoke. I didn't drink. I was an obedient and diligent student. What more could God expect? Still the doubts remained.

One day at school, Mr. Koops, our high school Bible teacher, was talking about Jacob and Esau in the Old Testament. Jacob and Esau were twin brothers, but the Bible says that God loved Jacob and hated Esau. I had always assumed that God loved Jacob because he was the better of the two brothers. But Mr. Koops said that if the choice were up to us, we would have chosen Esau instead of Jacob because Esau was a more likable person. Jacob was cunning and deceptive, the kind of person you could never trust. God chose him instead of Esau simply out of sheer grace and not because of any good qualities he saw in him.

But this went against my way of thinking. It didn't seem fair for God to ignore Esau's good qualities and to prefer his untrustworthy brother over him.

In 1963 our church had a new minister. Like Mr. Koops at high school, Rev. Jorritsma challenged my childhood assumptions. He insisted that salvation was completely a gift from God, not something we in any way earned or achieved. It was all about God's grace, not our own goodness. But this was a hard lesson to learn. My natural tendency was to trust in my own ability and goodness. What point was there in being obedient and staying on the honor roll if it didn't gain me any points with God? Wasn't there anything I could do to secure my status with him? Was he completely indifferent to all my best endeavors? It seemed there were always more questions than answers.

In the meantime, I continued to be an active part of the Christian community around me. At high school we had regular chapel services and classes in which we studied the Bible and church history. And I continued to attend church services and Catechism classes. Outwardly I was totally conforming to the expectations of the Christian community.

But inside there were still doubts. Did I really believe everything I was being taught? Could I trust God to love me and save me from the threat of sin and death and hell? Was I truly a Christian, or was I just conforming to the crowd around me so I didn't stand out and attract undesirable attention?

The time was coming for me to make a decision. Young people in our church were expected to make a profession of faith sometime in their teenage years. This meant they openly and publicly affirmed the Christian faith they had been taught since childhood. There were still questions in my mind with no answers. There were still doubts about how salvation really worked. But if I waited for complete understanding and absolute certainty, I would never move forward. I decided I was ready to make this decision.

In order to make a profession of faith, I attended a pre-profession class with six other young people. Since Rev. Jorritsma had already left our church and we did not have a regular pastor at that time, Rev. Cammenga, the pastor of the neighboring church in Drenthe, conducted this class. He prepared a list of thirty questions that summarized the Catechism teaching of the past several years. We were expected to be able to answer all of these questions satisfactorily.

Once we had completed this pre-profession class, we had to appear in front of the consistory to have our profession approved. The seven of us assembled in the basement hallway outside the closed door of our consistory room. We waited anxiously for the door to open. Finally, Rev. Cammenga swung open the door and invited us in. We stood in one corner of the room where all the assembled elders and deacons could see us. Rev. Cammenga asked each of us one or two of the thirty questions from his list, and we all answered as well as we could. Then a couple of the elders commented on how happy they were to see us. Next, they voted to accept our professions of faith.

A couple weeks later the seven of us sat together on the front pew of our church on Sunday morning, August 20, 1967. Rev. Cammenga read the form for the profession of faith from the back of our Psalter Hymnal. Then he asked us to stand, and each of us had to respond individually "I do" to a brief litany of questions, asking us if we believed in Jesus Christ as Savior, in the Bible as God's revelation to us, and in the church as the chosen community of God. When my turn came I pronounced my "I do!" loud and clear for everyone to hear. Now it was official. I had declared my faith to the world.

CHAPTER 6

STRIKING OUT

DURING MY SOPHOMORE year of high school, the Holland Christian School Society began constructing a new school building on a large campus south of the city. Instead of three compact buildings crammed into the middle of the city, this would be one sprawling building with long hallways, a large interior courtyard, and a huge gymnasium and band room all built on a large campus with expansive green lawns and extensive athletic fields. When I started my junior year, I attended school at this new building. We even had a cafeteria in which we could enjoy a hot lunch. The only problem was finding my way around such a large building. I got lost a few times that first semester.

Once I got used to the new school building, life in the classroom continued pretty much the same as it had always been. I studied hard to keep my grades up so that my name appeared on the honor roll. Sometime during that junior year I was chosen as a Junior Rotarian. I don't know who chose these Rotarians or what criteria they used, but I was proud to receive this honor. Four boys were chosen in the junior year and four in the senior year to attend a few meetings of the Holland Rotary Club. We received a delicious hot meal, talked with some of the businessmen and professionals at our table, and listened to a speaker.

At my last meeting, someone told me I would have to stand up and give a farewell speech. This was just a few minutes before it actually happened: so much for preparation! A boy from another high school, who spoke just before I did, gave a stirring speech about his ambition to someday become a permanent member of the Rotary Club. This provoked enthusiastic applause. Then I got up and mumbled something about my appreciation for the opportunity the Rotary had given me to be a part of their Club. I'm sure I didn't impress anyone with that speech.

Music also continued to be an important part of my life. My voice grew lower and lower as I matured during my teenage years, and soon I was able to sing a pretty impressive bass. So I became a member of our adult choir in church.

Later, my friend Jack decided it would be fun to form a young men's quartet, so he recruited me and two other teenage boys. Gladie Ver Beek, my mother's cousin, played the piano for us. We practiced frequently and sang several times at our church. Then we started getting invitations to sing at other area churches, so we sometimes became the featured special music at these services. I felt pretty impressive belting out the bass parts of such old Gospel favorites as "Prayer Wheel" and "Heaven Came Down."

One summer we were attending the Ver Beek family reunion consisting of all my mother's uncles and aunts and cousins, their children and grandchildren. We first ate a picnic supper at Spring Grove Park in Jamestown. Then we played a game of softball. I had a couple times at bat, but was only able to hit two ground balls. I was hoping for one more chance at bat, one more chance to really get a hold of that ball and send it over the left fielder's head, but the adults decided it was time to quit.

The next part of our evening centered on a home talent show. My sister Gayle and I were going to play a duet. We did not know the order of the program, so I sat down still sweating from my softball game to enjoy listening to a few other numbers, while cooling down and relaxing a little. Then the announcer for the evening promptly informed us that Dan and Gayle Boerman would start the program with their cornet and clarinet duet!

With visions of softballs and bats still dancing in my mind, I hurriedly grabbed my cornet from its case and walked up in front with my sister. I wiped my lips on my sleeve to remove the sweat before we began. After Mom had played a short introduction on the piano, Gayle and I started in. I hit most of the first notes okay, but as soon as the melody ascended to my upper range I sputtered and choked like a lawnmower running out of gas. I was supposed to play the top note while Gayle played a lower note of harmony, but she was forced to fill in some of the top notes when I collapsed. The whole performance was a disaster. Instead of hitting a home run on the softball diamond I struck out at the home talent show!

That same summer, on the Fourth of July, we were together with the Ver Beek family again, but now it was just Mom's brother and sisters, Grandpa and Grandma, and our cousins. Aunt Juella, in explaining why my cousin Norm was not in attendance, stated that he had gone with some friends to see a movie. I almost went into a state of shock when I heard this report. If this was not a deliberate succumbing to evil, then it was hard to imagine what would be! To walk consciously and deliberately into a movie theater was like sticking your bare hand into a swarming beehive. Everyone knew that movies were inherently evil forces and that the buildings where they were shown were dens of iniquity. What would you do if Jesus returned while you were sitting in a movie theater? Surely you would be in serious trouble! If I suspected the devil might be lurking in the shadows of a tent at the Allegan County Fair, I would not have been surprised to see him standing in full view collecting tickets at the movie theater. I did not attend a movie in a theater until *The Cross and the Switchblade* came out sometime later. I stood nervously outside the Studio 28 Theater, waiting to get in and wondering if I really belonged there. Even attending a movie with such an overt Christian message produced a lot of anxiety.

CHAPTER 7

ME AND THE MM

THE CO-OP WAS the tractor on which I cut my teeth learning to drive. Then for awhile we had an old Allis Chalmers. I don't remember driving it very much. It was a tricycle tractor like the Co-op. I always thought it looked like something a five-year-old kid put together; it was so simple and ugly. When we got rid of the Allis Chalmers, Dad bought a brand-new Minneapolis Moline Jet Star. The MM, as we called it, was a forty-four horsepower model with power steering and wide wheels on the front. It was the tractor I spent the most hours driving, and I formed a real attachment to it as to a trusted friend.

There were a lot of different tractor-driving jobs. Sometimes I used the manure loader on the MM to scoop manure out of the barn and load it on the spreader. I had fun trying to see how much manure I could get on a bucket. Then there was the trip to the field with the spreader, usually a pretty enjoyable job. But if there was a strong tail wind while I was spreading, I might get a few pieces of manure hitting me in the back as I spread. There was plowing snow in the winter and pulling wagons loaded with wheat or corn or hay from the field in the summer. There were the times I got stuck in a wet hole in the field and times when I got drenched by a sudden shower before I could get back home. But on the whole, driving a tractor was as close to Paradise as I got on the farm.

My favorite tractor-driving job was dragging a large field. Usually we did this on an angle so that the ground was not worked in the same pattern every time. To set the angle, I picked out a tree at or beyond the opposite end of the field and headed directly toward it so as to make a straight line. After this first time across the field, I simply followed the pattern I had established. The only hard part was turning around at the end, because I had to make a very sharp turn in order to resume dragging adjacent to where I had just been. If I turned too sharply, the drag could get caught on the rear tractor tire and be pulled up right onto the wheel. This could be a minor disaster. Fortunately, this never happened to me. We had a new twelve-foot drag that seemed enormous at the time. The MM cruised along pretty fast in third or fourth gear as it pulled the drag across the field. Taking a twelve-foot swath at a time, I rapidly transformed the field from a rough and sometimes weedy mess into a smooth, weedless landscape.

The purr of the MM's engine powered it across the field as I watched the lugs on its huge tires whir past me to meet the soil beneath them. The drag stirred up the soil to reveal its moist, pungent aroma as it waited for the wheat crop to be planted later in the fall. Flocks of grackles descended on the freshly tilled soil to pluck the exposed worms and grubs from the surface before they had a chance to burrow back into their secure home in the earth. The warm sunshine lit up my face as the cool breeze blew through my thick red hair. I sang some of my favorite hymns and popular songs as I powered my way across the field.

The MM and I shared many a happy hour together in Dad's fields. At the wheel of that powerful machine I felt pretty important and very much in control of the world. There was nothing quite like that feeling of control and freedom and unity with the fields and the crops that surrounded me. It was almost as much fun as flying.

CHAPTER 8

MOM'S GIFT

MOM CONTINUED SEEING different doctors to try to find relief from her frequent headaches, stomach ailments, and general malaise. In addition to medical doctors, she frequently went to Dr. Versandaal, a chiropractor in Holland. At one point Dr. Versandaal referred her to another doctor, who prescribed hormone therapy for Mom.

After one of her hormone injections, Mom came home and tried to relax. But instead of feeling more comfortable, she felt more and more agitated. Mom was sitting on the couch in our family room. She became so agitated that she began moaning and screaming out in her confusion and misery. I took turns with Dad and my two sisters in sitting by her side, holding her hand, and trying to assure her that she was okay. After awhile she gradually began to calm down, but it was obvious that Mom's hormone therapy was not helping. It seemed like all of Mom's attempts at healing ended up leaving her feeling no better than before.

Since Mom continued to struggle with her health and none of our local doctors were able to help her, Dad and Mom decided they should go to the Mayo Clinic in Minnesota to see if the doctors there could treat her more effectively. Dad drove Mom to Minnesota in February, and the hospital put her through an intensive series of tests.

While at the Mayo Clinic, Dad suddenly developed a blockage in his urinary tract and had to have emergency surgery on his prostate gland. So Dad and Mom both ended up as patients in the hospital at the same time. This prolonged their stay in Minnesota for a few days while Dad recovered from his surgery. The tests that Mom had did not show up anything specific that the doctors could treat.

During our parents' absence, Gayle and I were home alone on the farm. Bev was away at college. This meant that I had to get up early every morning to do the chores before getting ready for school. One morning as I walked to the west side of the barn to feed the pigs, I heard one of them screaming in distress. When I slid open the door, I saw the problem immediately.

The west end of the barn was lined with eight adjacent farrowing crates for sows and their little pigs. These crates were constructed of a heavy metal mesh. Each sow was confined between two parallel upright sections of this mesh, which were elevated about a foot from the floor and up to a height of about four feet. Beneath these upright sections was a wider area where the small pigs could walk around without the danger of being crushed when the sow lay down. These crates worked well to protect the small pigs and gave enough room for the sow to lie down and nurse them whenever she so desired.

One problem with the farrowing crates was that the sows could get their front feet into the mesh, climb up and sometimes jump out. In order to prevent this from occurring, Dad slid a couple of two-by-fours through the mesh above each sow's head so that she could not lift herself up and escape her confinement. Each board was secured in place with a large nail on each end.

On that morning one of the sows, in attempting to climb up the sides of her farrowing crate, had managed to get her head stuck between the two two-by-fours and was bellowing away in her distress. I grabbed a hammer Dad always had hanging in the barn and approached the sow in trouble. The closer I got the louder she screamed. Soon I was standing directly over the head of this three-hundred-pound animal emitting a deafening roar, while I struggled to pull out one of the nails from the two-by-four that had entrapped her head. After a few tries I got it out, pounded the end of the two-by-four, slid it sideways and out of the way, and the sow's head was free. She finally ceased her screaming, took her feet out of the mesh, and dropped quietly to the floor. Silence at last! I put the two-by-four back into a different position so she could not fit her head between them again, and pounded the nail back in to hold it in place.

I kept very busy doing all the chores plus keeping up on my school work as long as Dad and Mom were gone. Several families from our church invited Gayle and me over for dinner during this time so we didn't have to cook for ourselves all the time.

One Saturday while Mom and Dad were gone, several men from our community came over and helped me clean all the manure out of the part of our barn where we fattened our cattle. This was a large area of the barn, and cleaning it out usually took Dad and me several days. We had a manure loader on the front of our MM tractor and pulled the manure spreader with the Co-op. But on this Saturday we had several tractors and spreaders going at the same time, and we cleaned out the whole area in one day. I felt pretty important as I directed this undertaking and showed everyone where to spread the manure in the field. And it was exciting to get such a big job done so quickly.

I was relieved when Dad and Mom came back from Minnesota and I was no longer responsible for the farm. Mom, however, did not find any relief from her health problems as a result of her Mayo Clinic visit. She continued to struggle.

But there were also times when Mom had the courage and creativity to enjoy life and do positive things. One of her creative activities was writing poetry. Mom appreciated the beauty of the natural world and the joys of marriage and family life. Many of her poems are dedicated to these subjects. Autumn was her favorite time of year, and she describes the joy she felt in the autumn season in this poem entitled simply "Autumn":

> Oh, for the beauties of autumn!
> The trees in their finest are dressed.
> The earth, after giving much harvest,
> Is eagerly waiting for rest.
>
> The birds have all left for the southland,
> Awaiting the coming of spring.
> The pumpkins lie gold in the garden.
> The grain is all stored in the bin.
>
> The corn cribs are bursting with harvest,
> The cattle are safe in the stall.
> Thanksgiving is really in order
> To God, the great Giver of all.

Life was never easy for Mom, but she never gave up on it, either. Her poetry was the symbol of her desire to experience and celebrate the joy and the beauty of life. The sensitive and creative spirit that she expressed through her poetry is something that she also passed on to her only son. It is a gift that I will cherish forever.

CHAPTER 9

PLAYING FOR THE PRESIDENT

IN THE SPRING of 1968, at the age of seventeen, I volunteered to become a member of a Summer Workshop in Missions (SWIM) team. The SWIM program was organized by the Christian Reformed denomination to give young people a chance for a short-term experience of ministry. I was chosen along with five other high school students to help the Community Christian Reformed Church in Saginaw, Michigan.

There were four girls and two guys on our team. For six weeks Rog, the other guy on our team, and I lived with two different families of the church in succession. Most of the work we did centered around the church's Vacation Bible School (VBS) program. The first two or three weeks we spent a lot of time canvassing neighborhoods and inviting children to attend VBS. Then we spent a week organizing and helping to teach the children at VBS. When VBS was finished, we visited families who had sent their children to VBS and were interested in finding out more about our church. We also spent time studying the Bible together as a team and helping out with miscellaneous tasks around the church.

As we canvassed the area for VBS, one of the questions we asked people was, "What does this community need more of?" Most people talked about needing another park in the neighborhood or better police protection or something the city could do for them. But when I asked this question to one young black woman, she answered without hesitation, "I think this town just needs more love." I have never forgotten her honest and compelling answer.

One of the families Rog and I stayed with was a young couple with two small children. During our stay, their son celebrated his third birthday. Rog and I decided we should buy him a birthday present. Two teenage boys picking out a birthday present for a three-year-old was a huge challenge. We had no idea what would be appropriate, but we finally settled on a plastic dog on wheels that undulated up and down and made a barking noise when pulled with an attached string. On the evening of the birthday party, the three-year-old opened a couple of large, expensive gifts from his parents. After he had finished with them we were a little embarrassed to give him our cheap plastic dog. But he opened our gift eagerly, glanced back at his parents' gifts, and took off down the sidewalk pulling the silly barking dog behind him. Sometimes the novice really wins!

That fall I started my senior year of high school. During my Christmas vacation, Dad and I shared a harrowing experience.

It was December 31, 1968. Our church always had an Old Year's Service on the evening of December 31 to mark the passing of another year. As the afternoon passed into evening, the west wind began to blow with a rare fierceness that sent the falling snow flying past in a blinding sheet of white. Since my grandparents were the custodians at church, it was their duty to open up the building for everyone before the service. But as they watched the increasing fury of the storm outside, they decided it was no time for two seventy-year-old people to venture out. So they called us and asked if Dad could substitute for them that night.

Only Dad and I decided to attempt the journey to church that night. Dad edged the car slowly onto the road as we both stared intently into the dark, blinding fury of a blizzard. Dad cautiously proceeded down our road the three-quarters of a mile to the corner, where we turned and headed another half mile to church. No one else had arrived, so we began to turn on the lights and unlock the doors. We couldn't imagine that many people would come to the service on a night like this, but we wanted to be ready.

Rev. Van Schouwen, our minister at that time, noticed the lights of the church from across the parking lot in the parsonage where he lived. A few minutes after we arrived he walked over and told us the service had been canceled. So we turned off the lights, locked the doors, and headed back home.

The blizzard grew even worse. We made it safely over the half mile from church to our corner, but once we had rounded the corner neither Dad nor I could see anything. It was impossible to distinguish the road from the ditch. The headlights of the car revealed only sheer white moving in a horizontal direction.

Dad stopped the car. "Can you get out and try to figure out where we are?"

I got out, walked in front of the car, and peered ahead, trying to follow the light of the headlights to pick out any objects that would give me a clue as to where we were. After a bit of looking around, I caught a glimpse of some fence posts along the road, and the firm footing I felt beneath me assured me that I was walking on the road. I got back in the car, and Dad moved forward a little further. But soon we were both blinded again.

"Want me to get out again?"

"Yeah, I guess you better."

Once again I walked in front of the car to try to see where we were. This time I was able to catch a glimpse of a telephone pole and a snow bank on the edge of the road. We were still okay. Back in the car again, Dad moved forward a little further until we were both blinded again.

"I hate to do this to you, Dan, but I think you have to walk in front of the car and I'll follow you. You can see better out there, and I can see you in the headlights."

So I buttoned up my coat as tightly as possible and stood in front of the car once again. As soon as I got my bearings I started walking forward. I peered desperately into the white abyss, groping for any dark outlines of fence posts, weeds, snow banks, or telephone poles that would help me figure out where I was. As I walked slowly forward, I kept fearing that Dad might lose sight of me and run me over. But our desperate system of navigation worked all right. I could see better from outside of the car, and Dad could see me in his headlights.

We made our way down the road for about a half mile when Dad rolled down the window of the car and shouted, "It's okay! You can come back in now."

We had reached an area of our road which was partially sheltered by woods on the north side, and the wind and snow had slowed down significantly. We finally traversed that last stretch of road and turned with great relief into our driveway. It sure felt great to be back safe in a warm house again!

During my senior year of high school I became a member of the pep band for the first time. I enjoyed playing at our basketball games and helping to support the cheering effort of the fans. Our director, Mr. Vander Linde, had mentioned earlier in the fall that our entire band was being considered as a candidate to march in the Presidential Inaugural Parade in January, but none of us knew whether that was actually going to happen. During half-time of one of our basketball games, Mr. Vander Linde walked over to the announcer's microphone and stated that he had a special announcement to make. Before he could say another word, the entire pep band let out a raucous cheer. It was true: we had been chosen to represent the State of Michigan at the Presidential Inauguration in 1969! We would be part of the historic occasion of the inauguration of Richard Nixon, a man we then regarded very highly. This was indeed a high honor!

During the following weeks we practiced marching and learned the Michigan fight song from memory. When the time for the trip arrived, we piled into four buses and left for Washington, D.C. I had never been that far away from home before or participated in such an historic event. This was big stuff! On our way to Washington we stopped in Gettysburg, where the mayor gave us a personal welcome. The next morning we spent some time touring the battlefield. We stopped in Annapolis and attended church at the Naval Academy there on Sunday. We also spent a day visiting some of the memorials in Washington, D.C.

Finally, Inauguration Day arrived. We were bused to the appropriate location and began our march down Pennsylvania Avenue. It was a pretty cold day, and the first time we had to start playing, the mouthpiece of my cornet was so cold I couldn't get a sound out of it. But I warmed it up soon enough and was able to play fine after that. Someone who watched Richard Nixon on television told us later that he voiced the words "Good band!" as we marched past him. Whether he actually said that I don't know, but it was a popular rumor, anyway.

CHAPTER 10

GRADUATION

IT WAS THE spring of 1969, the last semester of my senior year of high school. The school year and my high school career were quickly coming to an end. No longer the scared little freshman of three years ago, I now strode the halls of Holland Christian High School with confidence and pride. I considered myself a young man in secure control of his own destiny. I had been accepted at Calvin College in nearby Grand Rapids and was anticipating my start of college in the fall.

Two events of that spring still stand out in my mind. One was the honors luncheon held on June 9 at Jack's Restaurant in Holland. Along with thirty-two other graduating seniors, I was invited to this special luncheon that paid tribute to the Honor Students of the Holland Christian High School Class of 1969. From our high school we all boarded a bus that transported us to the banquet room at Jack's Restaurant. There we enjoyed chicken salad, rolls, chips, fruit Jell-O, and ice cream. Mrs. Kruithof, one of our English teachers, entertained us with a lively book review of a biography of

Marie Antoinette. One of my classmates played a piano solo and three others joined for a woodwind trio. It was a celebration of four years of high school study successfully completed.

The second outstanding event was my final high school chapel service. Various students took turns leading such services, but I had never done so until that day. Usually two students shared this responsibility. One led us in singing a couple songs and in prayer. Then the second student gave a brief meditation. But for reasons I cannot recall, on this occasion I was chosen to lead the service by myself.

Our principal, Mr. Holwerda, introduced me by saying, "Responsibility for leading our chapel service today rests solely on the broad shoulders of Dan Boerman."

I stood up and announced the opening song. At first my voice quivered a little, but as I sang I grew more confident. After another song and a brief prayer, I opened my Bible to the Old Testament book of Ecclesiastes. There I read the well-known words from chapter three:

> For everything there is a season, and a time for every
> matter under heaven:
> a time to be born, and a time to die;
> a time to plant, and a time to pluck up what is planted;
> . . . .
> a time to love, and a time to hate;
> a time for war, and a time for peace.

Then I reflected with my fellow seniors on the four years we had shared together in high school. There had been good times and bad, new things learned and times when we failed, new friendships made and times when we were shunned by classmates, basketball games won in overtime and other games lost by twenty points. But through it all we had grown to become stronger and more mature young people. Through it all God was guiding and blessing us.

After I gave my meditation, Mr. Sprik, one of my teachers, complimented me and said that my comments showed a lot of potential.

My high school days were now over. I had survived all the lonely walks in the halls, the Algebra exams, the gym classes, the fear that kept me from asking a girl out on a date, the long nights of study at home, the excitement of a tournament basketball game, the thrill of marching in a Presidential Inauguration—all the good and bad experiences of high school were over. And I was a better and stronger person because of them.

I was excited and ready to go forward with my life. The new challenge and adventure of college beckoned.

I was spreading my wings.

I was ready to fly.

WinePressPublishing
Great Books, Defined.

To order additional copies of this book call:
1-877-421-READ (7323)
or please visit our website at
www.WinePressbooks.com

If you enjoyed this quality custom-published book,
drop by our website for more books and information.

www.winepresspublishing.com
"Your partner in custom publishing."